PRAISE F

"Divinely Queer opened my e
Best tells her story so honestly that by the end of reading this book, I felt that she and I were dear, old friends. This type of storytelling is exactly how our world can be healed - one story at a time. Make this one of the stories you hear." - *Grace M., A Lover of People and God*

"I found it to be raw, uplifting, poignant, insightful, and reaffirming. For LGBTQ folks who have struggled with reconciling their sexuality and spirituality I recommend adding this to your must-read list immediately. It captures Jennifer's journey and spirit." - *Willie B., Spiritual, Queer Man of Color*

"I was moved to tears, moved to celebration, and moved to spiritual connection over and over as I read through this written expression of Jennifer's journey. I believe the world needs this book. I believe it was divinely directed and I'm so eager to see how God works through it to reach people with His love." - *Lavonne J., LGBTQ Ally*

"Jennifer Miracle-Best shares a message of love that is unequivocally poignant and perfectly timed. Her courage to share her life in such a personal and intimate way is inspiring and brings hope to so many who may feel lost. *Divinely Queer* will show us all, whether LGBTQ+, ally, or those who have questions, how to bridge the gap between spirituality and sexuality. There are many more beautiful things to come from this gifted author." - *Megan S., Survivor of Spiritual Violence*

"Being someone who identifies as both Christian and lesbian, I have often questioned my choices as well as the repercussions for those choices. Reading this book gave me desire to reconnect with my faith as well as eliminate many guilts and concerns. The ability to read someone's memoir who has walked in my shoes, questioned the things I've questioned, and experienced the feelings I've felt is a blessing in and of itself. These words hold importance that will mold faith and self-acceptance while saving so many lives. Beautifully done." - *Jess C., Lesbian & Recovering Southern Baptist*

"Divinely Queer is captivating, enlightening, and relatable. It is a must-read for any member of the LGBTQ community who has ever questioned their spirituality and whether God loves them. Jennifer's journey is proof that sexuality and spirituality are interrelated, and that the ability to love - regardless of gender - is truly a gift from God." - *Paul M., Deacon, Metropolitan Community Church of Detroit*

DIVINELY QUEER

My Journey to Spirituality Through Sexuality

Jennifer Miracle-Best

Divinely Queer: My Journey to Spirituality through Sexuality
Copyright © 2018 by Jennifer Miracle-Best

VoicePenPurpose Publishing, voicepenpurpose.com
Columbia, MD

Some names and locations have been changed to protect privacy.

Cover Photo: Emily Marie Haase Photos
Cover Design: James, GoOnWrite.com
Page Design: Amy R Brooks, VoicePenPurpose Publishing

Jennifer is available for keynotes, discussion forums, and book talks in person and remotely. Visit JenniferMiracleBest.com to contact her.

Discounts for bulk purchases by nonprofits, schools, corporations, and other organizations may be available. Write to *Jennifer@JenniferMiracle.com* to inquire.

Material excerpted from the book *The Little Soul and the Sun* ©1998 By Neale Donald Walsch, used with permission from Hampton Roads Publishing Red Wheel/Weiser, LLC Newburyport

DEDICATION

For all of the Beings who came before me and shined their Light for the World regardless of the consequences. Thank you for inspiring me and so many others to shine our unique Light.

For all of the Beings who came with me and shine their Light for the World with mine. Thank you for continuing to Light the Way when some of our Lights go dim. May we return the favor when you need an extra Spark.

For all of the Beings who will come after me and shine their Light for the World. Thank you for your fearlessness and your courage in the face of fear. May you see the day that all Darkness ceases.

CONTENTS

Finding God

I am.

I am a Being who shares my authentic Self with others. I share my experiences and my knowledge in order to expand the Universe, to expand others' perspectives, understanding, and knowledge which will, in turn, expand their own experiences, Life, and Universe. I chose to come here to help to raise the Consciousness of the Earth and everything I think, say, and do is to that end. Inspired by the Light of so many others, I shine a different Light in the World that not everyone can see, but those who do will feel Grateful & Inspired to see a glimpse of themselves and to be ignited to Shine their own special Light that may be a little more like those who couldn't see My Light, and they will Inspire those who see Their Light to Shine in the way I have Inspired those who saw my Light and so on and so on and eventually, all the World will be a bright, beautiful, brilliant Light so powerful that all Darkness will cease and we All will experience Ecstasy.

- JMB, October 17, 2016

PREFACE

The first time I felt the power of God, it felt like magic. In fact, I think it took me a minute to even realize what had happened. It was the morning that my uncle was coming to help me load up all of my earthly belongings to move four states away. For the job of my dreams, I was moving to a town where I knew no one, and had nowhere yet to live. It was the job I'd been dreaming of and working toward for more than three years. Everything about the interview and campus visit had felt right, yet I woke up that morning with an overwhelming sense of anxiety. I had an irrational fear that I was in over my head and that I had somehow fooled them into hiring me. I would later learn this actually has a name - imposter syndrome - and impacts many of us in different ways throughout our lives.

On this morning, my heart was heavy with fear and anxiety. So much so, that I called an ex-girlfriend, who had already made a big move herself, for some encouragement. She tried to assure me that what I was feeling was normal, that she had experienced some fear too, and that I would be fine once I got there. Although I appreciated her effort, it did not calm my fears. We hung up and I forced myself out of bed to begin getting things together.

I found that I couldn't even function because of this overwhelming emotion and the sound of my internal voice asking, "What have you done?" At some point, before I could even get dressed, for the first time in my life, I found myself on my knees, forehead to the floor, overcome and sobbing with fear, anxiety, and loneliness and praying for God to "calm my heart."

Let me be clear - this was not a conscious decision to suddenly give prayer a try. This was literally an involuntary act of desperation. My mind and body simply had no ability to do anything else. I can't tell you how long I was there on the floor, but all of a sudden, I had this realization that I felt calm. I didn't feel great. I wasn't all "Awesome! Let's move to Georgia, today!" but indeed, my heart felt calm. I felt good enough to get up and function and do what had to be done. I also had a brief moment of realization that I had just prayed to God and that God had provided me with exactly what I asked for…and that felt like magic.

Up until that point in my life, I had never had what I understood to be a "God moment" as I sometimes call them now. In fact, for a good part of my adult life, I wasn't sure I necessarily even believed in God. After all, what kind of God would reject me for loving the wrong person as my dad had insisted was the case? For a long time, it was much easier to dismiss my father's beliefs as bullshit than to actually try to reconcile my sexual orientation with what the Bible - which was never read in my home - supposedly says about who can love whom and to what degree.

If you would have told me in 1995 that someday I would be writing a book about my connection with God, I would have called you crazy. More accurately, I would probably have rolled my eyes at you and dismissed your comment as some hope for my soul's salvation, which I was totally not interested in. However, I've since come to understand, that despite being told I was unacceptable to God and unlovable by Him because of my identity; in fact, the opposite is true.

It is *because* of my sexual orientation that I have uncovered my divine connection to Spirit and I am writing this book to share my journey with everyone in the world who still feels the way I did twenty-two years ago. Unfortunately, I know for a fact that you're out there. And there are a lot of you.

I want you to know that you are exactly who you were created to be. God makes no mistakes. We all have a Purpose and a Calling and everything about us is a tool for delivering our gifts to the world. I want you to read my story and to recognize that you, too, have experienced the power and love of your Creator in your life and that you are not only worthy of God's love, but you're *made* of it! It's *why* you were created! I hope that you come to realize, as I have, that nothing and no one can separate you from God. It is impossible because we are *made of God*. The Life Force that moves our blood through our veins and causes our heart to beat and our lungs to breathe involuntarily...that's God. God is *in* us and we cannot be separated from the Divine. We can, however, choose to be intentionally connected to and conscious of the Divinity within us. And when you are connected with the Divine, you can be, do, and have everything your Soul desires.

***

INTRODUCTION

My whole life has been a Journey to this book. There have been all kinds of twists and turns and clues along the way, but perhaps the brightest light on my path was a children's story written by Neale Donald Walsch called *The Little Soul and The Sun*. This parable introduces readers to the concept that, at our core, everything and everyone is simply a different aspect of the same beautiful bright Light. This simple story helps both children and adults understand that we are all different, unique, and special in our own way. Our uniqueness never makes us better than any other being; simply different. We cannot be better than any other being because essentially, we *are* every other being. We are all the Light, which is everything.

For me, the most compelling part of the story is the idea that we all come into this physical life with the intention of having a particular experience. Once we have decided on the experience we intend to have during our human journey, other Souls agree to come along and help us create it.

In the story of *The Little Soul and The Sun*, the Little Soul tells God that he wants to have the experience of forgiveness in his next lifetime. After God explains that all of his creations are perfect - angels, in fact - and that there is no one to forgive, another Soul comes forward. This Friendly Soul offers to come into the Little Soul's next life and do something for the Little Soul to forgive. Understanding that in order to do this, the Friendly Soul would have to pretend to be something he is not, the Little Soul is overcome by the Friendly Soul's generosity and asks why he would offer to do such a magnificent thing for him. The Friendly Soul explains that he will do it out of love for the Little Soul.

Remembering how he will have to "forget himself" and pretend really hard to be something he is not, the Friendly Soul asks the Little Soul for one thing in return:

"Remember Who I Really Am."

"Oh, I will!" cried the Little Soul, "I promise! I will always remember you as I see you right here, right now!"

"Good," said the Friendly Soul, "because, you see, I will have been pretending so hard, I will have forgotten myself. And if you do not remember me as I really am, I may not be able to remember for a very long time. And if I forget Who I Am, you may even forget Who You Are, and we will both be lost. Then we will need another soul to come along and remind us both of Who We Are."

"No, we won't!" the Little Soul promised again. "I will remember you! And I will thank you for bringing me this gift - the chance to experience myself as Who I Am."

And so, the agreement was made. And the Little Soul went forth into a new lifetime, excited to be the Light, which was very special, and excited to be that part of special [interactions] called Forgiveness. And the Little Soul waited anxiously to be able to experience itself as Forgiveness, and to thank whatever other soul made it possible. And at all the moments in that new lifetime, whenever a new soul appeared on the scene, whether that new soul brought joy or sadness — and especially if it brought sadness — the Little Soul thought of what God had said.

"Always remember," God had smiled, "I have sent you nothing but angels."

FINDING ME

CHAPTER ONE
Mum's the Word

Having grown up in a family with Southern Baptist roots, to say it didn't go well when my parents found out I was in a relationship with a woman would be an understatement. Maybe "roots" is too strong of a word, as it kind of implies strong ties and that certainly was not the case. I did not grow up in what most would describe as a religious home. My mom, sister, and I attended church sporadically, most memorably at Easter and Christmas. We did not pray at home - even before a meal - and we never read the Bible. In fact, I'd never seen my dad in church a day in his life, but the Bible was the very first thing he brought up the day that he figured out I was dating a woman.

In the spring semester of my freshman year of college, I had the opportunity to do an internship at Walt Disney World. Although I had gone away to college the previous fall to a campus that was about two hours from home, I knew that my parents were still pretty easily accessible should I need anything. So, moving to Orlando for a semester was kind of a big deal. It was my first time truly being on my own.

During the thirty-minute drive to the airport I had this

unfamiliar feeling of anxiety. As my mom would tell it for years, I'd always been the kid that would go anywhere with just about anyone. For the first time that I could remember, I felt scared and nervous about going so far away. We sat at the terminal gate at Detroit Metro Airport, my mom on one side and my dad on the other. As we waited for boarding to begin, I had a huge lump in my throat and was holding back tears. I had only flown one other time in my life and never alone. I felt like if I said anything, the dam would break and the tears would fall. I can still remember how I was trying to keep it together during those last moments. Before I knew it, the flight attendant was calling my zone to board the flight.

"That's you," my mom said and my heart dropped.

"But, I'm not ready…" I said, and there went the dam.

I could hold back the tears no longer. I remember hugging both my parents, but especially my dad. I can still hear him reassuring me that I was going to be okay. Little did he or I know how dramatically my life was about to change over the next six months. I also had no way of knowing that that moment was the last time I would ever experience this kind of love and reassurance from my dad.

A lot happened during my time in Orlando that semester, including getting engaged to my boyfriend, Les. This huge decision came in a close second in significance only to me falling in love with Tawnny, a woman nine years my senior. Yes, these two very conflicting events happened within the five months that I was away on my internship.

It didn't take long after I returned home from Disney for my dad to surmise that I was in a relationship with Tawnny. It must have been late May or early June of 1995. Within days of arriving home, I had broken off my engagement with my fiancé and couldn't stop talking about the possibility of transferring to a college in Florida, so that I could continue to work at Disney World. I had danced competitively since I was a young girl and it had always been my dream to do it for a living. Before leaving Disney, I had auditioned to be a character in the parks and had been selected but did not have the means to pay for my living expenses for the rest of the summer. So I came home with every intention of transferring and going back to the "happiest place on earth" as soon as possible.

I had a conversation with my dad in the garage one afternoon shortly after I arrived home from Florida. The garage was my dad's sanctuary. It was a detached garage that he had commissioned some friends to build and it was huge - especially next to our 900 square foot home. He had started working on cars when he was just 13 and seemed to know everything there was to know about them. It was not uncommon for him to do work on cars that belonged to our extended family and friends as a kind of side-job. This afternoon, he was working on the 1968 Camaro that he and his best friend had decided to build from scratch. I went out to talk with him about breaking off my engagement. I'd already determined it was what I needed to do and had brought the subject up with both of my parents as something I was thinking about. However, I was still looking for their validation while at the same time trying to figure out how to do it without raising too many red flags.

"Being offered the opportunity to work as a character at Disney just really made me realize that there are lots of things that I want to do before I think I'll be ready to get married," I said to my dad as he continued to work under the hood.

"And you know, with the Disney College Program, all I have to do is work one day per year to stay on their payroll!"

"Oh, yeah?" my dad said, not looking up from what he was doing.

"Yeah! Isn't that cool?! I mean, I'd really love to transfer to school down there and be able to work at Disney while I get my degree, but I really have no idea how that works, so even just going back to work once or twice a year would be great until I can figure it out," I rambled on. Getting no audible response from my dad, I carried on. "I just feel bad, because I really don't want to hurt Les, but I just don't think I'm ready to get married."

"Look, if you love him, and you know you want to marry him, and there's not a doubt in your mind, I support you one hundred percent," my dad said. "But if there is one *iota* of doubt...I am *one hundred percent* against it."

He finally stopped whatever he had been tinkering with as he delivered that second sentence, shifting his focus directly to me as if to ensure that I understood the gravity of what he was saying and the conviction with which he was saying it. I felt relieved to have his support in that moment, even if I knew he wouldn't support the source of my doubt if he knew the truth.

It seemed the breaking off of the engagement and my obsession with going back to Disney World in and of themselves did not immediately tip my dad off about my relationship with Tawnny. However, add to that mix the fact that I was talking to Tawnny daily, sometimes multiple times a day, and well...I think he started to do the math. At the time, I truly never, ever, expected him to actually figure out what was going on between us. Needless to say, I was pretty much blindsided the day he confronted me about the nature of our relationship.

I don't know where my mom and sister were, but it was an afternoon that my dad and I were home alone. The conversation was prompted by yet another call from Tawnny. This was way before the days of everyone having a cell phone, so he was well aware of her calls and many times was the one to answer them. This time was no exception.

"It's for you again," he said as he handed me the phone and I immediately knew it must be Tawnny.

"Hello?" I said, wondering why she was calling me again so soon. She was well-aware of the situation with Les and that I had no intention of telling my parents what was going on with her. I wanted to head into my bedroom with the cordless phone, but also worried my dad would think that was weird. We'd just hung up maybe an hour earlier, after an hour and a half conversation I'd already taken in my bedroom. Instead, I stepped into our kitchen which was still in earshot of my dad who was sitting on the couch.

"Hi. I'm sorry, I know we just talked a little bit ago, but I was just thinking about you and missing you and so...I just wanted to call and tell you I love you," she said.

"Okaay..." I said with a smile, feeling like my dad was listening to every word.

"Your dad's sitting right there, isn't he?" she asked.

"Yeah," I confirmed.

"Can't you go to your room?" she asked.

"Not right now, no," I replied hoping she would get the hint that I was really uncomfortable and just wanted to get off the phone.

"Okay...well...maybe you can call me later?" she asked.

"Maybe," I said in an upbeat tone thinking more about how it was sounding to my dad than to Tawnny.

"Alright...I hate this," she said.

"I know," I said, again making a point to sound like I was enthusiastically agreeing with something she said rather than sympathizing with what she'd said.

"Okay, I hope to talk to you later," she said.

"Me, too," I replied.

"I love you," she said.

"Okay, talk to you later!" I knew that she understood why I didn't mirror the sentiment, but also felt badly about it.

"Bye," she replied before hanging up.

"Bye," I said as I hung up the phone and headed back through the living room toward my bedroom.

Before I could get there, my dad took this opportunity to ask me more about Tawnny. Although he had met her very briefly the night my family arrived in Orlando to pick me up at the end of my Disney program, there was not a lot of conversation between them and he had never asked about her again. Until now.

"That was your friend, Tawnny, again," he said, as more of a statement than a question.

"Yeah." I replied, nervous about saying the wrong thing but still not really thinking he knew what was going on between us.

"You two talk an awful lot. Doesn't she have a job?" he asked.

"Yeah, Dad. We worked together at Disney. That's how I know her," I laughed, trying to make the conversation feel more comfortable and throw him off my trail.

"Isn't she quite a bit older than you?" he asked.

"Yeah, I guess...like, nine years?" I replied, feeling more nervous with every question. "But, you know I've always been 'thirteen going on thirty' as Mom always says."

"You don't think it's odd that she calls you so frequently?" he pressed.

"No," I said as I shook my head with a shrug. And then he was done beating around the bush.

"Do you think she might be gay or bisexual?" he asked.

My parents having raised a kid who could not lie, I sheepishly answered, "Yes…" reasoning with myself in my head that answering that question truthfully said nothing about me or our relationship, clearly not anticipating his immediate follow-up question: "Do you think she might be interested in you?" To which my response was a silent, deer-in-headlights expression met with the immediate follow-up to the follow-up: "Or is that what's already going on?"

Here it was. The moment of truth that I did not see coming. Did I mention I'm a horrible liar? In that moment, I was unable to say no, but also unwilling to say yes. Unfortunately, my silence spoke volumes. I wish I could remember the exact words my dad said once he recognized the truth in my silence, but I don't. At this point I simply remember sitting on the couch directly across the room from him, listening to him go on and on about how wrong it was.

"Do you know what the Bible says about that?!?" he asked, in a tone that implied *he* did. However, up to that point in my life he had never shared it with me. I had no recollection of ever talking about the Bible at all, much less what the Bible said about anything in particular. So I really had no idea what - if anything - the Bible said about that. "It's ethically wrong! It's morally wrong! It's wrong in the Bible!" he went on as he paced the short distance from our couch to the doorway of our kitchen. "I don't even know who you are! *My* daughter would never do something like this."

I sat silently. I didn't know what to say. I had never been on the receiving end of such condemnation, especially from my dad. Finally, he told me, "If you go to Florida, you're on your own." With that, I escaped to my bedroom and cried. A few minutes later, my dad opened my bedroom door and clearly as an afterthought said, "If you don't decide to go to Florida, we don't need to tell your mom about this. It would just upset her." With that, he left me alone in my room.

I was completely heartbroken by my dad's ultimatum and his shaming words. I didn't know what to do. I had always done what my parents told me to do. For the first time in my life that was significantly at odds with what I wanted and, although I wasn't fully aware of it yet, it was ultimately at odds with Who I was.

So, I did what a lot of people do when they don't know what to do. Nothing.

I was stuck living at home until late August when classes would begin. I was working part-time at the local hospital where both my mom and dad worked. For the most part, we carried on that summer like nothing had happened, but things were never the same between me and my dad. I had a sense of security in not having to talk about it when I was home because I knew that my dad would not bring up the situation in front of my mom. However, I felt anxious when I would run into him in the halls at work. You know that feeling you get when you've just flown by a cop on the highway? That same feeling of dread permeated my body every time I saw him in passing. My stomach dropped, my heart pounded, and then slowly I'd feel the tingling dissipate throughout my body as it tried to get everything back to normal. All this was happening on a physical level while I also tried to avoid any kind of conversation.

It didn't help that on a couple of occasions he actually brought up the subject. One day, after weeks of awkwardness between us, he invited me to have lunch with him at work. As we were eating lunch together and I was trying to act like there wasn't a huge elephant at the table with us, he pointed right to it, expressing his concern about the fact that I'd finally told my ex-fiancé the truth about why I had broken up with him.

"Les told me you told him about her," he said with no warning. My heart dropped into my stomach and I suddenly wasn't hungry. I nodded.

"Do you think that was a good idea?" he questioned. I stared back at him silently.

"What if he tells Joe?" he pressed, referring to my cousin, who had introduced me to Les.

"I asked him not to tell anyone," I replied.

Clearly that hadn't worked because he had obviously told my dad. At the time I really thought this whole conversation was all about my dad's shame of my behavior. Later, I would wonder if it was more about his fear of my mom hearing about the situation from someone other than him, especially since he had been aware of it for weeks.

I spent the rest of the summer working and dodging my dad whenever I could. I spent a lot of time out with friends or away from the house whenever my parents were home in an effort to avoid awkward interactions with them. If you've ever kept a secret from someone, you know how uncomfortable it can be to try to operate as if everything is normal. I think I've already established I'm a horrible liar, so it was much easier to just avoid the whole situation. In an effort to ensure it did not come up when my parents were home, I worked out a system with Tawnny that I would call her phone, let it ring once, and hang up. This let her know it was safe to call my house without my call to her showing up on my parents' phone bill. It was a temporary situation until I could get back to campus where I would have the freedom to talk with her whenever I wanted. I thought the fall semester would never come.

CHAPTER TWO

Learning About Boys

Growing up, I'd only dated boys. Two, to be exact. By "only dated" I mean, that's the only purpose they served in my mind. I'd only ever been socialized to think of boys as off limits until I was old enough to get married - which, by the way, was decidedly not until I turned thirty-five.

Anytime there was any kind of interaction with a boy, I was made fun of, always by male family members. "Oooh, Jennifer has a boyfriend," my dad's brother would tease anytime there was a boy around or mention of a boy, regardless of the nature of my relationship with him or my age. This happened as early as grade school and I always felt embarrassed and uncomfortable about it. So, the concept of having friends who were boys was foreign to me. However, that's precisely what made my first boyfriend so endearing.

From seventh grade through my junior year in high school, I dated Tony. To this day, Tony is one of my dearest friends and one of my favorite people. Although I would come out to him about my relationship with Tawnny years before he finally came out to me, we have come to understand that we had a bit of a *Will & Grace* relationship. By that I mean, we were drawn to each other because we were safe for each other. He wasn't interested in having sex with me and, although I didn't know then that I wasn't interested in having sex with him, I think I felt comfortable with him because we were best friends and there was never any pressure to be anything more. Eventually, however, we both would feel that pressure from peers.

During the summer before our junior year of high school, Tony broke the news to me that he'd gotten drunk at a party and slept with some other girl. We had lived in different towns since our freshman year in high school and only saw each other on the weekends. Although some of my friends claimed to be sleeping with their boyfriends, he and I had never even discussed it. Based solely on the idea that my friends were already having sex, I began to wonder why nothing like that was happening between me and him. Like most women who have been socialized to think about these things, I wondered if there was something "wrong" with me. Then he dropped this bomb. I was devastated. However, I also felt his genuine remorse and realized that he could have easily kept it from me, given the circumstances. So, when he asked me to forgive him, I did. We continued dating for almost another year, but still he expressed no interest in becoming more intimate than we'd been to that point. Being the "good girl" that I was, I was not about to be the one to make a move. So we carried on as usual, laughing and listening to music, and playing games together, and making out from time to time, but never anything more intimate than that.

In the spring of my junior year of high school, I stood in my cousin's wedding. As an official bridesmaid, I was invited to several parties in preparation for the big day. Although he wasn't in the wedding party, my cousin's friend Les attended some of these pre-wedding festivities. Like my cousin, he was four years older than me and the only single guy at the party. It was the first party I'd been to where there was drinking that seemed almost permissible because my family was with me. I had a few drinks throughout the night and Les gave me the kind of affection I had been curious about for a long time but had never received from Tony. I liked it. I liked it so much that, after nearly four years, I broke off my relationship with Tony and began dating Les.

Les was your stereotypical "man's man." He drove a pickup truck, shared a love of cars with my dad, and he lived for bowhunting season. He had a full mustache which made him appear older than he was, smoked about a pack a day, and his hands were perpetually stained with oil from working on forklifts at his job. He was the quintessential polar opposite of Tony. In retrospect, I think my dad seemed to understand the contrast between the two on a whole other level than I did at the time. I remember glimpsing tears in my dad's eyes as my dad reacted to my news that I intended to break up with Tony.

"That's too bad. Tony's a good kid," he said as he carried on with the task at hand in his garage. "I never had to worry about you when you were with him." Whether it was what he meant exactly, or not, I interpreted that statement to mean that he never had to worry about me being pressured into sex.

Les and I dated throughout my senior year of high school. On Christmas of 1993, he gave me a promise ring. Even then, like most girls my age, I loved the idea of being the object of someone's affection, but it still felt weird for him to give me this ring in front of my parents. Admittedly, I didn't understand the potential implication of the ring, only that it signified a commitment to our relationship. While he quickly clarified that it was a promise ring - not an engagement ring - I never, especially in that moment, anticipated that there would be an engagement ring. At that point, marriage felt like a lifetime away, something I would probably do some day, but definitely not in the next four years.

However, when I arrived in Orlando for my semester internship at Walt Disney World, one of my favorite roommates was the first person I met who was my age and was already engaged. She was from Oklahoma with an adorable Southern accent and a beautiful solitaire engagement ring. Although it was a surprise to me to meet someone my age who was committing to marriage, it didn't take long for me to be swept up in the romanticism of being engaged. By the time Les came to visit me and surprise me with a proposal, I had been perfectly primed. Or at least primed enough to get caught up in the romance of the moment and override the overwhelming anxiety I was feeling in my body as he placed the ring on my finger. With the decision to commit the rest of my life to someone, there was this sense of dread knowing that I was making a decision that felt so final, yet, there wasn't really a reason to say no. Who'd ever heard of a woman being proposed to and saying no? Clearly at the age of nineteen, I didn't get that the dread I was feeling *was* the reason to say no. I also had no idea I was about to fall in love with a woman.

CHAPTER THREE

The Happiest Place on Earth

Falling in love with Tawnny was not a story of love at first sight. In fact, I don't even remember the first time I met her. At first, she was just a friend I worked with at one of the retail locations at MGM-Studios. We had a lot of fun working together because our personalities seemed to just click. Before we even knew each other very well, we often knew what the other was going to say and sometimes would even finish each other's sentences. We had what I recognize now as a strong energetic connection that felt magnetic. I would look forward to the shifts that we were scheduled to work together, but initially, that was the extent of our relationship and I had never thought anymore of it.

One afternoon, my friend, Abdel and I joined a group of other co-workers for a lunch break at one of the backstage staff restaurants. As we sat down, they were talking about a female co-worker. It was a large table and it was loud in the restaurant so I was only getting bits and pieces of the conversation. The bits I did hear confused me because it seemed they were talking about this woman having a girlfriend who worked in one of the other parks. I was sure I was misunderstanding the situation because the woman they were talking about was gorgeous by anyone's standards. She had long brunette hair, beautiful skin, and her makeup always looked natural but flawless. *'She couldn't possibly be a lesbian,'* I thought. Later that night, as Abdel gave me a ride to my apartment after our shift, I decided to ask him about it.

"So, I'm confused...at lunch today, were they talking about Samantha?" I asked.

"Yes," Abdel replied in his Moroccan accent.

"I totally thought I heard them say something about her having a girlfriend. Did I understand that correctly?" I asked.

"Oh, yeah. She's a lesbian. Her girlfriend is Jessica, the manager in strollers at Magic Kingdom," he said, very matter-of-fact.

"She is??" I asked in astonishment.

"Yeeeeah!" he replied in a tone that communicated that I was clearly the only person to whom this was news.

"Wow! I never would have guessed that about her," I said, still trying to wrap my mind around this new information. I'd never met anyone who I knew was gay and the only representation I'd ever seen was on television talk shows which only portrayed lesbians as manly.

"Oh, yeah! You do realize that something like 65% of Disney cast members are gay or bisexual, right? It's like, the gayest place you can work," he laughed.

"Really?? No! How would I know that?! How do *you* know that?" I said, intrigued yet still not sure I believed him. "Are you serious?"

"I'm totally serious!" he laughed at my disbelief. "Disney is known for being one of the most gay-friendly employers in the country. Why do you think they call it the happiest place on Earth?" he said, with a wink.

"Huh. I had no idea," I said, still feeling perplexed.

"Yeah, she's not the only one that we work with who is gay. There's another person that I know of who is at least bisexual," he said.

"Really?? Who??" I asked instinctively, fascinated at this point and genuinely curious about this new world I seemed to be living in. Suddenly realizing just how sheltered and ignorant I seemed to be about the subject at hand and sensitive to the privacy of others, Abdel hesitated.

"Umm...I don't think that's something I'm supposed to tell you," he replied, soundly genuinely uncertain but almost like what he was really saying was that he didn't think it was something I was supposed to ask.

"Oh, yeah! Of course. Sorry," I replied, immediately getting the cue and feeling embarrassed that I didn't know better.

"No worries! It's okay. You didn't know. I just think it's like, they'll tell you if they want to tell you, you know?" he explained.

"That makes sense," I replied as we pulled up outside my apartment building. I thanked Abdel for the ride home and headed inside.

I found myself fascinated with this new information he

had shared with me. Over the next several weeks, I would find myself wondering about which co-worker Abdel was talking about when he said that he knew of another person who was at least bisexual. I played this game of process of elimination in my head that is so ridiculous for me to think about now. For example, I eliminated at least one co-worker as a suspect because she was "too old to be a lesbian." Others I dismissed as a possibility because they were married, oblivious to the fact that someone could be bisexual and be married. Ultimately, I could never narrow it down because there were too many people that I worked with that I didn't know well enough to "figure it out." Although I could not definitely eliminate her based on whatever uninformed criteria I had determined made sense to me, I thought I knew Tawnny well enough to know it wasn't her.

Around that same time, I had begun to spend time with Tawnny outside of work. The first time we hung out together started with dinner and a movie. We had tons of easy conversation as we often did at work, but I did not perceive it as romantic. After the movie, she told me she wanted to take me somewhere else that was a surprise. Just minutes from the cinema, we pulled up to a storefront that belonged to a psychic tarot card and palm reader. I'd never been to a psychic before, so I was intrigued. However, I thought I was just along for the ride until Tawnny told the woman that we would both be getting readings.

"Oh, I didn't realize…" I started to explain that I didn't

have the money for the reading when Tawnny interrupted me.

"Oh, no - it's my treat," she said.

"Are you sure?" I asked, feeling a little uncomfortable about her paying for my reading.

"Yes! It was my idea," she insisted as the psychic led me into a separate room for my reading.

"Would you like to know the good and the bad, or only the good?" the woman asked as we sat down at a table where she began to lay down tarot cards.

I was caught off-guard by this question. Initially, I thought, *'who comes to a psychic to get bad news?'*, but ever the optimist and unsure of how much I really believed in this stuff anyway, I figured, *'how bad could the bad news really be?'*

"I want to know everything," I replied, enthusiastically.

Out of the thirty minutes I spent with this psychic, there are two things that I distinctly remember from the reading. The first was, "there is someone who cares deeply about you, but isn't telling you." This just seemed like such an odd thing to say or know about someone. I felt puzzled by it. It almost felt like code for "you have a secret admirer." The other was, "you will lose a close family member in the next year." My skeptic brain felt like these both seemed like rather vague things to say that could potentially happen to anyone. However, I would be lying if I said I didn't start thinking about my grandparents and wondering if there was something going on at home that I didn't know about.

I experienced several nights out with Tawnny before I began to seriously contemplate whether she might be the "mystery bisexual person" I'd been trying to identify. We'd spent a lot of time together and she'd shared a lot with me about her family and other personal things about herself and I just never really got the impression that it was necessarily her - but I also had not completely ruled her out. However, having already dismissed that possibility for the most part, it was a comment from a roommate after learning I was going to hang out with Tawnny yet again that put her back on my radar.

"Do you think she might like, *like* you?" my roommate asked with a facial expression that clearly said, "Ew."

"No," I said, dismissively. However, on the inside, I was perplexed. I had not even mentioned to my roommate anything about my hunt for the mystery bisexual person at work. '*What made her say that?*' I wondered… '*and what if she's right?*'

The day that I returned to work with an engagement ring on my finger provided the first indication that perhaps my roommate was on to something.

CHAPTER FOUR
Forbidden Freedom

It was sometime in late February or early March, several weeks after I had begun frequently hanging out with Tawnny, that Les proposed during his visit. The first day that I returned to work wearing an engagement ring, my shift started before hers and I had been there a couple hours when she arrived. I had subtly shared the news of my engagement with other co-workers in the context of casual conversations about how my visit with Les had gone. This, however, created much excitement with co-workers who were happy for me and making quite a big deal about it, showing off my ring to other co-workers as we encountered them. Then, in walked Tawnny.

I was behind the counter with a co-worker, working the register when she arrived. There was another co-worker on the opposite side of the desk admiring my ring and asking for details. Tawnny noticed us gathered around as she came in from backstage. The co-worker who was behind the counter with me waved Tawnny over.

"What's going on over here?" she asked, smiling and curious.

Without saying a word, I put my left hand out on the

counter in front of her, fingers spread wide, displaying my ring. She stared at the ring for a few seconds before looking up at me. I watched the joy leave her face as the realization of what it was set in.

"Congratulations," she said as she forced a reluctant, tight-lipped smile. "I've gotta go clock in," and she headed toward the back room.

The shift in her energy was palpable. Even though it was clear that she did not share my excitement, it didn't exactly occur to me that it was because she had feelings for me. One of the things she had shared with me was that she struggled with and was being treated for depression. I allowed myself to believe that she was just having a difficult day and gave her some space. A few days later, when we worked together again, things seemed to be back to normal, reinforcing my theory.

Tawnny and I continued to spend time together outside of work, further developing an emotional bond. After work, I would often go with her to her house where she lived with her mom, and we would go to the local movie theatre or just hang out at her house and spend the evening talking. I loved spending time with her, but still there was nothing physical happening between us. Nor were there any awkward or uncomfortable interactions or anything alluding to a romantic relationship.

A few weeks later, we planned a weekend trip to Sanibel Island. Tawnny had taken a trip to visit her ailing grandmother who lived in the Midwest. She was very close with her grandmother and I had heard a lot about her. While she was gone, Tawnny had left her car with me to use for the week and when I picked her up from the airport, we headed directly for Sanibel Island for the weekend.

It was a long drive and we talked the whole way there. I heard all about her visit and some more about her family. We had dinner at a well-known restaurant that was right on the beach and then headed back to our inland motel for the night. As we sat in the quaint motel room and continued to chat, Tawnny became noticeably uncomfortable as she told me there was something she wanted to tell me.

"There's something I want to tell you, but…oh my gosh…I'm so nervous," she said as she took a deep breath and released it. In that moment, I immediately knew what she was going to tell me. I think there was a part of me that was just as nervous to hear what she had to say.

"Okay…" I said, quietly.

"I just really don't want anything to change between us," she said, hesitantly.

"Okay," I replied again, this time more matter-of-factly.

"I'm just gonna say it," she said followed by a long pause.

'I really wish you would,' I thought to myself. I really wanted to let her off the hook and just tell her I knew what she was trying to tell me. I also knew that I couldn't tell her I knew what she was trying to tell me because I was afraid she would think that our friend, Abdel, had told me. So, I did my best to

try to make her comfortable to just say what she needed to say.

"It's okay," I said to her reassuringly.

"I'm bisexual," she said, watching me intently for a reaction.

"Okay," I said and smiled at her.

"Okay? That's it? You're not going to run out of here?" she asked, sounding relieved.

"Why would I do that?" I asked.

"I don't know, I just...I don't know!" she laughed, followed by another deep breath and release. I laughed equally out of nervousness and relief. "So, we're okay? You're not mad?" she asked.

"No, I'm not upset at all," I replied.

"Well, say something!" she said after a long pause, clearly still anxious about what I was thinking.

"What do you want me to say?" I asked, laughing and genuinely unsure of how to respond.

"I don't know…" she replied, still watching me for my reaction. "Like, do you have any questions about it?"

Although I knew immediately when she said she had something to tell me that it was going to be that she was bisexual, I truly did not see it coming until it was happening. I only knew it in that instant. While I hadn't completely ruled her out in my process of elimination I'd been playing, I also had not concluded that it was her until the very moment that she spoke the words "there's something I want to tell you."

So, I truly had no idea what to say. I absolutely had not prepared for this moment in my mind. Yet, I did find myself curious about it, so I decided to take the opportunity to ask some questions.

"When or how did you know?" I asked.

"Well…" she started, relaxing a bit as she opened up about it. "I guess it was probably in middle school." She went on explaining how she had memories of finding other girls attractive and how she explored that and what it meant for her. I followed up with questions about how her family reacted about it. She spent the next hour or so talking about her revelation. I sensed that it may have been the first time she'd had the opportunity to really open up about it with anyone.

Eventually our conversation wandered back to work, her family, and her trip to visit her grandmother. She filled me in on the details of her grandma's health and it was not looking good. She was very worried about her. Feeling the weight of her emotions about her grandmother, she said to me, "I don't want to think about my grandma anymore, right now. Let's talk about something else."

At this point, we were laying side by side on one of the beds, both staring at the ceiling as we were talking. The question that I wanted to ask but didn't want to ask kept swirling in my mind.

"Jenny, say something to take my mind off my grandma," she said after a few minutes of silence.

I held my breath for a minute and then finally asked, "Are you attracted to me?"

After a moment of silence, she replied "Well, I'm not thinking about my grandma, anymore!"

We both laughed but then the weight of the question hung in the air between us. "I tried really hard not to be," she began, "because I know that you're with Les and you're not available, but...yes."

Only then did I find myself wondering why I asked the question and even regretting I asked, because now I felt obligated to have some kind of response. I heard the words and said them over and over in my head until I finally made them come out of my mouth, "I wish I felt the same way about you...but I don't." The moment the words left my lips, I wished I could take them back. There was a heaviness that hung in the air between us for a moment as Tawnny took my statement in. Without another word, she got up from the bed we were both lying in, turned out the light, and got into the other full-size bed.

I knew, in that instant, everything had just changed between us. I found myself wishing I hadn't said it but knowing I had to. I was engaged and I needed to be clear. What I didn't immediately realize was that I was setting that boundary for myself, not for her.

When I woke up the next morning, Tawnny had already showered and was packing things up to get on the road. She was also still clearly upset about what had transpired the night before.

"Good morning," I said to her as she came out of the bathroom, her hair still wet from her shower.

"Morning," she replied without making eye contact.

Sensing that I was getting the cold shoulder, I took every opportunity I could find to try to engage her in conversation.

"Have you been up long?" I asked.

"Since about 6am," she replied, carrying on with what she was doing.

"Wow! That's early," I replied, but got no response. After a few minutes of silence, I tried again, "Want to get some breakfast before we go?"

"I'm not really hungry," she replied, still not stopping to make eye contact or direct her response toward me.

I did my absolute best to act like everything was totally normal. But it wasn't, and she wasn't about to let me pretend that it was. We got into the car and headed to a gas station to fuel up and grab some snacks for the three hour drive back to Orlando. I made a few more attempts to get Tawnny to talk to me, but all she would give me was the bare minimum response. The silence just during the ride to the gas station was deafening and I found myself on the edge of tears with frustration by the time we stopped. I gave up on trying to act like everything was okay.

"Are you mad at me?" I asked as we got back in the car after getting snacks.

"No, Jenny, I'm not mad at you," Tawnny calmly replied.

"Okay...so...why aren't we talking?" I asked as I felt tears well up in my eyes. She continued to pull out of the gas station and get back on the road.

"I'm sorry," she began after a long pause. "It's not your fault...I knew that you were not available, and I really thought I had my feelings in check, but...hearing you say that last night just really hurt."

"I'm sorry," I said as I felt the tears spill onto my cheeks.

We drove for miles before she spoke again, "I feel like a different person when I'm with you." There was a long pause as I took in her words and she seemed to search for the words to further explain her feelings. "You've made me feel things that I haven't felt in years. It's like you've woken up parts of me I didn't think were there, anymore. I've never felt this way with someone before."

Hearing this evoked more tears from me as her words resonated with what I had felt. We drove on in silence as the tears now streamed down my face.

"Talk to me," Tawnny finally said, invitingly, after several miles of silent tears.

My mind was reeling as I tried to process the emotions I was feeling. Her words, "I've never felt this way with someone before," resounded in my head and my heart. I recognized that I felt the things she was feeling, too. I also recognized that this was going to be a problem for me so I found myself afraid to speak it. The thoughts, fears, and emotions swirled in my mind until I felt like I had no choice but to let them out of my body.

"As soon as I said what I said to you last night, I wished I hadn't said it," I began to speak through my tears. After a long pause, I continued, "because I do feel the way you feel. I've never connected with someone the way I have connected with you. I mean, we literally finish each other's sentences. It feels so amazing, so natural...so *right*," I began and then paused as thoughts of why this is so scary to speak out loud ran through my mind. "Then, I think about my family and how they would react if they knew how I feel about you...or even the rest of the world, and how it's viewed...and I can't understand it. What could be wrong about feeling this way? How can something that feels so right, possibly be so wrong?" I asked through a fresh wave of emotion.

Tawnny reached over and took my hand in hers for the first time. It was a new level of intimacy that I'd never experienced with her or any other woman. It felt simultaneously forbidden and freeing. Her touch was gentle but intentional and comforting. It was if a new layer of me opened up as I felt a wall I didn't know I'd been keeping up, come down. As we drove for a while in silence, my hand in hers, it felt like there were no need for words. Eventually, we continued our conversation, discussing not so much specifically our feelings for each other as much as our thoughts about our feelings and the way it is received in the world. We never really came back to our specific situation in terms of the feelings between us and the fact that I was currently engaged to someone else. However, as we arrived back in Orlando, we'd definitely reconnected on a deeper level.

That night I stayed at her house. The couch in the living room pulled out into a full-size bed where we sat up talking into the wee hours of the morning. We sat, side by side, both leaning against the back of the couch facing the opposite wall. When there was a natural lull in the conversation, I asked Tawny what she was thinking.

"I'm wondering what it would feel like to kiss you," she replied, still looking straight ahead. Feeling a flutter in my chest, and somehow still caught off guard despite the conversation we'd been having literally all day now, I was still processing what she'd just said when she turned and looked at me and asked, "May I kiss you?"

In that moment, my heart shut down my brain and any thoughts of what anyone else might think, feel, or do about it and as my eyes met hers, my head involuntarily nodded yes. My breath felt caught in my chest and my head felt light as she slowly leaned in, bringing her lips softly, but firmly to mine. My whole body felt tingly in a way that had never happened before as one kiss led to another and before we knew it, we were passionately making out in the full light of the living room while her mother slept in the other room. Eventually, as the rising sun was coming in through the front window, we fell asleep with the living room lights still on. This would be the first of many nights that we would spend together. Over the weeks, our relationship would continue to deepen and reach new levels of intimacy. We dreamed of plans for me to transfer to an Orlando-based university, continue working at Disney, and find an apartment together.

Although I was still in contact with Les occasionally via phone calls, I had not told him about what was going on between Tawnny and I. My plan was to have a face-to-face conversation with him when I got back to Michigan. However, I never intended to tell him - or my parents - about my relationship with her. I anticipated it would not go over well with any of them and thought it would be best to explain our breakup as a realization that I was just way too young to settle down and had too many things I wanted to do in life before I was ready for marriage - all of which was also true. Between my dad's intuition and my inability to lie, this plan would be foiled. It ended up being a very long summer.

CHAPTER FIVE

It's Not You, It's Me

Eventually I realized that, regardless of what happened with me and Tawnny, I was not going to marry Les. Despite my clarity, I waited until I returned to Michigan to break off our engagement. Initially, I went with the old "it's not you, it's me" approach, which as cliché as it sounds, was totally true. However, that initial conversation would not be our last. Understandably, he was confused and heartbroken about it and asked to come to the house one day to talk. At this point, my dad had already confronted me about Tawnny, but no one else knew anything about my relationship with her, including Les.

"Being offered the opportunity to work as a character at Disney just really made me realize that there are lots of things that I want to do before I think I'll be ready to get married," I explained to him as we sat together on my daybed in my bedroom. This had been my consistent go-to line for my mom, my dad, and now Les.

"I understand...but it's not like we're getting married tomorrow. Your dad's condition on his blessing was that we don't get married until you're finished with school," Les replied. "So, there's plenty of time for you to do lots of things."

"I really want to do whatever I can to try to make a career out of dancing. I want to travel. I want to transfer to school in Orlando so that I can work in the parks while I finish school," I said, suspecting this would be a big enough deal breaker that there would be no alternative but to go our separate ways.

"What if I went with you?" he replied after a moment of contemplation.

Fuuuuuck, I thought to myself.

"Les. You don't want to move to Florida. You hate the hot weather. You love bowhunting, which I imagine there's not a lot of down there. Besides, what about your job?" I argued.

"It's a national company. I can see if there are any job opportunities down there," he replied. It was becoming evident that I was going to have to tell him the truth. I'd done everything I could to avoid it and I'm a horrible liar, so I had no other option at this point. I took a deep breath and let it out.

"I didn't want to tell you this," I began.

"Tell me what?" he asked, tilting his head slightly. I held my breath and my stomach was full of nerves as I tried to figure out what to say. This was not at all how I saw this conversation going.

"I...kinda met someone else," I said.

"You met another guy," he said, in an of-course-you-did

kind of tone. "Now, it's all making sense," he continued, shaking his head as if he couldn't believe he hadn't figured it out on his own.

"Well, not exactly," I replied.

"I'm confused," he said which was clear from the look on his face. I took another deep breath and let out a long sigh.

"You know my friend, Tawnny, who I've mentioned to you a few times?" I asked.

"Yeah…" he replied, still clearly confused.

"I just, really connected with her," I struggled to find the words to explain our relationship.

"So…you're dating a woman?"

"I mean…yeah, I guess you could say that," I said, feeling both relieved to have it out in the open, but equally anxious about where this conversation was going.

"Wow," he said, still looking perplexed and taking a moment to process the information.

"I really didn't want to tell you," I said. There was a long silence before he spoke again.

"How did this happen?" he asked. "I mean, how do you just all of the sudden decide you like women?"

"Well, I don't know if I know the answer to that. I don't know if I would necessarily say that all of the sudden I like women. All that I really know is that I like this woman," I replied. There was another long silence.

"Have you guys kissed?" he asked.

"Do you really want to know the answer to that question?"

"Yes," he replied.

"Yes."

"And you liked it?" he continued with his questioning. I hesitated, still nervous about the direction of our conversation.

"Yes," I finally replied.

He paused, perhaps contemplating how much he really wanted to know before asking, "Did you sleep with her?"

The ball of nerves in my belly seemed to be expanding as I contemplated whether to answer his question. Ultimately, given the fact that I had cheated on him while I was in Florida, I felt like the least I could do is be honest about it now.

"Yes," I replied.

"Did you like it?" he pressed.

"Dude!" I said, giving him a look of disapproval.

"What? I mean, I was just gonna say invite her over!" he said, only half-jokingly.

Annoyed, I sighed, "No. That's not how it works," I answered in a serious tone. "It's you, or her, not both at the same time."

"Oh, *now* there's rules," he said, pointedly. I deserved that.

We'd come to a place where there really wasn't much more that could be said. Given the circumstances and the various ways in which he could have reacted to the kind of news I'd delivered, Les was incredibly calm. I think he was more hurt than anything else. Knowing that I was the one hurting him felt horrible. However, it also felt like, on some level, he fully understood that it wasn't about him or anything he'd done and so, perhaps that made it easier for him to not react in an aggressive way.

Knowing that he was still close with my cousin who had introduced us, I asked that he please not discuss this with anyone. I told him about how my dad had reacted to the news and that my mom was unaware of the situation and implored him not to speak a word of it to anyone. He agreed and went on his way.

CHAPTER SIX

If I'm Wrong, God Strike Me Dead

I moved back to campus without having another conversation with my dad about Tawnny. He may have assumed that since I had not brought it up again I had decided not to move to Florida and that might be the end of it. The truth of the matter was that I was a first-generation college student who had no clue about how transferring worked, and given the circumstances, I put those aspirations on the back burner.

When I returned to campus after a summer of dodging my dad and conversations about Tawnny, I met Mary Beth Pope. Mary Beth was my English 101 instructor. She provided a space for me to process what was happening in my life at a time when I felt like there was no one else in my world like me. As a frame of reference, this was more than a year before Ellen DeGeneres' famous coming out episode on her sitcom, *Ellen*. Beyond musicians k.d. lang and Melissa Etheridge, there were virtually no out, visible celebrities at the time.

In this class we did a lot of autobiographical and personal writing. We also did a lot of peer editing. However, Mary Beth offered to the class the option of having her as our editor if we were writing about something we were not comfortable sharing with our peers. There were multiple assignments in which I wrote about what was happening in my life - either about Tawnny and/or about my relationship with my parents. These assignments provided me such a valuable opportunity to process my feelings.

Mary Beth provided me with so much support, taking the time to talk with me outside of class and being the only person in my immediate environment that I felt safe to talk to about my situation. She also referred me to the campus counseling center which I had no knowledge of prior to my interactions with her. Although it seems like a simple thing, her influence significantly impacted the trajectory of my life. By simply listening, caring, and providing love and support, I'm convinced she changed my life in ways that she, and maybe even I, will never truly understand.

When I went to the campus counseling center, I was met with openness and acceptance. Again, this may not seem all that surprising in today's world, given the strides that have been made politically and in terms of social acceptance, but 1995 was a whole different world. I would continue to see my counselor throughout my time as an undergraduate. My positive experience with the counseling process not only got me through the next three years, but would enable me years later to feel comfortable seeking therapy again as I struggled with depression. In fact, I would spend a good portion of my adult life in therapy working through the various emotions that came up along my Journey to finding Who I Am.

Early in the semester, Tawnny planned a trip to come and visit me in November. As fate would have it, my mom called and let me know that she and my aunt were going to be coming to Mount Pleasant the same weekend. Shit. I knew the time had come to finally bring my mom into the loop.

One weekend in October, I traveled home to work as I often did. This time, I had written a letter to my mom in which I shared with her what had been going on in my life over the last several months. I told her about the nature of my relationship with Tawnny, the fact that Dad had known about it for months, and that he specifically told me to keep it from her. I also told her that Tawnny was going to be in town the same weekend she was planning to visit. I still invited my mom to come, but knew that I had to share with her what was going on.

I took the letter home with me to deliver that weekend, but could not seem to find the courage to give it to her until I was leaving. In fact, I almost didn't give it to her then, either. I went to my truck with the letter still in my pocket. As she was seeing me off, my dad was inside on the couch watching TV. At the last minute, after she'd closed the front door, I got out of my truck and went back inside. Pretending to have forgotten something, I headed into my bedroom and once inside I called her to my room. When she came into the room, I gave her the letter and told her to read it when Dad was not around and to call me after she'd read it. Clearly caught off guard, she took the letter and simply said, "Okay."

I headed right back out the door and drove what felt like the longest trip of my life back to campus. Monday came and went. Tuesday came and went. By Wednesday, I began to think my mom wasn't going to call me, ever. It was Thursday before I finally got a call from her - one I was both anxiously awaiting and dreading at the same time.

"I guess I just don't understand how you can feel that way about a woman. Do you think maybe it's because you didn't have a mother figure there?" she wondered.

'Ew.' I thought. "Mom, no," I replied. "It has nothing to do with that. I fell in love with her the way you fall in love with anyone."

I had to give my mom credit. It seemed to me she was at least trying to understand rather than going immediately to judgment and condemnation. She asked questions to understand the situation before ultimately saying that she wasn't going to disagree with my dad. She also announced that she and my aunt would not be visiting that weekend. The weekend came and went and that was the end of it until I went home for Christmas break when shit would really hit the fan.

At the time, Disney had a policy that Walt Disney World College Program alums could stay on their payroll by working just one day per calendar year. Since I was still holding onto the dream of someday returning to dance in their various shows, and of course, planning to stay with Tawnny, I booked a trip to Orlando for the first week of January before spring classes would begin. I intentionally booked it before I went home for the holidays, because I knew that if I waited I would cave to the pressure of my parents and would not do it.

As I had done with my mom months before, I wrote my dad a letter to break the news that I would be making a trip to Florida. I waited until after Christmas to give it to him because I didn't want to somehow be responsible for ruining Christmas. I knew that he would think the trip was all about Tawny. So, I made a point to explain to him that while I was indeed going to visit Tawny, more importantly, I wanted to maintain this opportunity to work for Disney. Not surprisingly, he wasn't having any of that. He was livid. But, because I had a sister who was 14 at the time, and "do you know what this would do to your sister?" they waited until New Year's Eve after my sister had left for a sleepover at a friend's house to finally approach me about the situation together. It would be the first and only conversation about my relationship with Tawny, to be had between me, my mom, and my dad.

I was getting ready to meet my best friend at another friend's house for a party when my mom came into my room and summoned me to the living room. The conversation did not go well.

"Can't you just stop talking to her? Maybe if you ignore it, it will go away," my mom suggested.

"No, Mom. It doesn't work that way. Besides, even if I did, how do I know I won't fall in love with another woman someday?" I replied.

"What if someone told you that you couldn't be with Mom?" I asked my dad. "Would you be able to just stop loving her?" I tried to reason with him. He wasn't having any of that, either.

As I sat crying on the couch in our living room at the front of the house, I could hear my dad, whom I'd never seen cry in my nineteen years of life, hopelessly sobbing from the back room of our tiny little home.

"She doesn't know what she's doing," I could hear him desperately crying to my mom, as if he meant that I didn't understand the consequences of my actions.

He would eventually pull himself together and come back to the living room to berate me. He said terribly hurtful things that made me feel unloved by him, but worse, unlovable by God.

"I always prayed you'd never come home and tell me you were pregnant, but I wish that's what you were telling me. I'd rather you were strung out on drugs or killing people because that can be rehabilitated!" he declared. "If I'm wrong, God strike me dead!"

Up until this point in my life, I felt like I'd always been kind of a golden child to my parents. I followed all the rules and was really good at school. I loved to learn and I loved to please people. I was in the concert band, on the pom-pom squad, in honors classes and brought home good grades. It seemed there was nothing at which I did not excel. I was an obeyer. I did everything my parents asked me to do. In the past, hearing my father sobbing about what a terrible thing I was doing by loving another woman would typically have been more than enough to compel me to cut off all communication with her. The fact that I was refusing to do so in that moment should have been a huge, blinking, neon sign for me that this was a defining moment in my life's journey. Of course, I was nineteen at the time and so overwhelmed with the heaviness of such rejection that it was only in retrospect, years later, that the profoundness of that moment would sink in for me.

Eventually I would come to recognize this experience with my parents as my first test of Consciousness, the first major event in my life that would begin to show me Who I Am. By that, I mean that my unwillingness to simply obey my parents' wishes as I typically did, was not based in rebellion or even an undying love for Tawnny. It simply did not align with my Spirit to deny this love I was feeling just because others did not understand or approve of it. In the same way that they could not begin to understand my love for another woman, I could not begin to understand how anyone could be so opposed to my love for another woman. How was my loving another person harmful to anyone or anything else in the world? How could something that felt so right, be innately wrong as my parents were telling me? Years of life experience would help me understand that my conviction about the situation was a gift from God - that it was rooted in a Truth that would eventually set my Soul on fire and become a passion that would lead me to my Calling.

Ultimately, my parents and I came to a stalemate. I was not going to convince them that night that what I was doing was okay and they were not going to convince me that it wasn't. When this became evident to everyone and it seemed there was nothing more to be said, my mom came back into the living room. I noticed immediately that she had left my dad, still distraught, in their bedroom at the back of our small house.

"Well, if you're going out, I guess you better go," she said. It was now 11:30pm on New Year's Eve heading into 1996. I was still in a bit of a fog from all that had transpired, but I quietly got my coat from our tiny coat closet in the hallway and headed out to join my best friend, Jenny, at a party at a mutual friend's house. I arrived just as the clock was about to strike midnight. Happy fucking New Year.

The next day my mom summoned me again from my bedroom. This time my dad sat on the couch, staring intently at the TV - the way that feels intentional in order to avoid conversation. My mom began to undress the Christmas tree. Standing in the doorway that separated our tiny kitchen from our equally small living room, I felt the anxiety of another conversation like the one we had the night before sitting heavily on my chest.

"Audie?" My mom said my dad's name as if to simultaneously get his attention and invite him to start the conversation. His eyes never left the television. He shrugged and nodded in her direction as if to say, "You do it."

Looking a little frustrated about his unwillingness to engage, she appeared to take on the responsibility of speaking for both of them.

"Well, your dad and I have talked about it and we realize that you are an adult and you're going to do what you're going to do," she explained as she continued removing ornaments from the tree. "We cannot make your decisions for you. You have to live with your decisions, and we don't want to know any more about it unless you're telling us it's over."

A silence hung in the air as I held my breath, waiting for the other shoe to drop. After the dramatic expression of emotions the night before, I had imagined all sorts of terrible outcomes including being put out of the house indefinitely. I stood there in the doorway, processing what she had said and regaining a more regular heart rate as I began to realize that things might actually be alright.

"So, would you like me to take you to the airport tomorrow?" My mom asked, interrupting my thoughts. Her tone was almost chipper. This was perplexing given the gravity of the conversation we'd just had. Had she really just offered to drive me to the airport immediately after condemning my reason for going in the first place?

"Uh...no...thank you...Jenny is going to take me," I

replied.

"Okay, well, can you get me a sweatshirt from Disney while you're there?" she asked. *What...the...?* I thought.

"Sure," I replied.

CHAPTER SEVEN

It's Complicated

After things came to a head with my parents that New Year's Eve of 1995, I returned to campus feeling a lot of different things. I felt relieved that my parents had not disowned me and that I had the freedom to make my own decisions. At the same time I felt shame about disappointing my parents in what felt like the worst possible way. I felt confusion about who I was and what my attraction to Tawny meant about me. I felt alone and invisible in that I did not know *anyone* else who was in the kind of relationship I was in. It was during this time that, although I was still in a long distance relationship with Tawny, I also began spending time with Jake.

Jake was a friend that I danced with in the dance company. He was handsome and a couple years older than me. He was not your typical "man's man," but you may have guessed that based on where I met him. Jake was super laid back and seemingly non-committal in a way that felt very comfortable for me, given that I was technically in a long distance relationship with someone else. Unlike my past relationships, there was not this instantaneous sense of committed monogamy. Even as we continued to see each other more frequently, there seemed to be a consciousness about not moving too fast or jumping into things. The things we did jump into did not necessarily hold the weight of obligation that others, myself included, might have expected them to. At one point, I experienced some dissonance because of feeling, on one hand uncomfortable with the uncertainty of whether he was spending time with other people the way he'd been spending time with me, and at the same time, hoping he was not expecting me to not be spending time with other people the way I'd been spending time with him. It was a loose, interesting dance that allowed me to continue to explore my sexuality without the obligation of disclosing my relationship with Tawnny...until she came to visit.

A few days before Tawnny was to arrive, I went to Jake's room to have the talk. I was so anxious and uneasy about it. After all, I had never given him any indication whatsoever that I was in any kind of relationship or even that I was interested in women. I had, however, mentioned that I had a friend coming to visit me from Florida. She was coming to visit the weekend of our spring dance concert, so I knew there would be no way to avoid our paths crossing. Although it was not Jake's style to interact with me in mixed company in a way that indicated to anyone that we were more than friends, we had been spending a lot of time together privately, and I wanted to remove any possibility of Tawnny finding out about that. I've already thoroughly established the fact that I cannot tell a lie which meant it would be completely obvious if I was uncomfortable around Jake.

I went into the conversation expecting it to be incredibly uncomfortable and to not end well. From my perspective, I hadn't been honest with him from the beginning about the situation and that was completely unfair to him. I had never lied about anything, but I had omitted information that, at that point, I felt I owed him. I fully anticipated losing that relationship and was ready to let it go before I would let go of my relationship with Tawnny. Much to my surprise and relief, Jake was a saint.

"So...my friend that's coming to visit me from Florida..." I said, cautiously followed by a long pause.

"It's a guy," he guessed.

"No...but, it might as well be..." I replied with a wince.

"Ah..." Jake said with a knowing nod as he realized what I was getting at.

"I'm sorry. I should have told you. I didn't know what to say. Or when to tell you. Things have been kind of undefined between you and me..." I began to try to explain through my tears.

"So, you're a lesbian?" He said in a way that felt more like he was asking for confirmation than necessarily an open-ended question.

"Honestly, I don't know. I mean, I met Tawnny while I was at Disney last year and I love her. But she's 1200 miles away and my parents kinda lost their shit about it which has made it very hard to feel good about." Through tears, I went on to tell him more about my dad's reaction in particular and Jake held me as I cried.

He shared with me that he had dated a girl a few years earlier who was bisexual and that it was okay. Everything was going to be okay.

"I'm going to give you all the space you need this weekend," he said as he looked directly into my eyes as if to ensure I was understanding. "I want you to take all the time you want and need with Tawnny. I will not call you this weekend and I don't want you to feel like you need to call me. If you need or want to talk, I will be here for you, but I will leave the ball in your court."

I was so incredibly grateful for and humbled by his grace, especially given the circumstances. There were no strings attached, no ulterior motives. Just pure grace. Grace that I had not received from my own family. I was overcome with emotion that I'm not sure I had ever felt in a state of gratitude before.

That weekend would come and go and I would not tell Tawnny about my relationship with Jake. She traveled back home to Florida and we continued our long-distance relationship, staying in touch via phone calls and snail mail through the spring semester. When I returned home at the end of the semester, our correspondence was more limited due to my parents' disapproval of the situation.

It was shortly after I returned home for the summer that

we got the news that would ultimately change our family forever.

CHAPTER EIGHT
Careful What You Wish For

At the end of the 1996 spring semester, I went home again to work for the summer. In addition to my job at the hospital, I had taken a retail job at the mall. During one of my first days at that job, I received an overhead page. The call was from one of my mom's five sisters letting me know that my dad had been admitted to the hospital. She said he appeared to have some internal bleeding that they had not been able to identify or explain. Immediately panicked, I left work and went directly to the hospital to figure out what was going on. When I arrived, my dad was upset that I was there.

"I told them not to call you," he said as I walked into the room. He knew that it was the first few days of training for me at my new job. Additionally, much like most men in my experience, he didn't want anyone fussing over him. Particularly, not me. However, my mom and my sister had gone on a day trip by bus to Holland, Michigan, for the Tulip Festival and would not be back until later in the evening. So, he was stuck with me.

It was super awkward. Yet, now there was this mutual concern for his health which directly conflicted with his masculinity. He insisted that he was fine and didn't need me there with him.

Although his hospital stay ended up being short, the tests and medical visits would continue for over a month. Eventually he was diagnosed with colon cancer. We had no family history of cancer - colon or otherwise - of which we were aware. It was a Friday in mid-June of 1996 when my parents shared the news with me. I found myself standing in that same doorway where I had held my breath on New Year's Day as my mom delivered their position on my life choices. I held my breath again as my dad delivered the news. I felt my eyes immediately well up with tears as my dad told me that he had cancer. Seeing my tears, he immediately addressed them by laying out the plan that he would be having surgery on Monday and that should reveal more about his prognosis.

"Like I told your mom, let's not get upset until we know there's something to be upset about," he said, reassuringly. At that moment I decided he would never again see a tear fall from my eyes. I thought to myself that if he can be this brave, I had no right to shed a tear in his presence. And I never did.

Over the next five months, he was in and out of the hospital a handful of times. It's hard for me to remember his symptoms and the details of exactly what happened with each visit, but I remember my mom frequently being very emotional about it. This was unusual for her and I was frustrated by it. I interpreted her tears as defeat. Despite his ninety-pound weight loss, lack of appetite, and struggle to eat, I was in complete denial.

"He's thirty-eight. People live forever with cancer," I would say to my best friend, Jenny. But, my dad wouldn't live forever.

I think it was during his initial stay in the hospital after having had surgery to remove as much of the cancer as they could that, although my feelings for Tawny had not changed, I realized I could no longer be with her. I sat by his bedside while he rested, an NG tube running through his nose, down his throat, and into his stomach to feed him. Things had never been the same between us since the whole conversation about my relationship with Tawny. We'd never spoken about it again after that New Year's Day when my mom let me know they didn't want to know anything else about it unless it was over. I yearned to be close to him again, especially as I contemplated the idea that, as far as I knew, the cancer could kill him. As I sat silently with my dad, I said to myself in my head, "You've always been with boys. You can be with boys. If being with boys will make him happy, I will be with boys." It was almost as if I was giving myself some kind of weird pep talk. In that moment, I made up my mind. The problem was, I did not communicate it to Tawny.

I spent the rest of the summer distancing myself from her, knowing that I had the excuse of not being able to openly communicate with her because I was living at home and all that was going on with my dad's health. While there was a part of me that felt like a breakup conversation needed to happen in person, I knew that there was also a part of me that did not want to break up with her. It was August or September when I finally initiated the conversation with her. She was flying through Detroit on her way to visit her family in Ohio, and she had a layover that was a few hours long. While this was still not an ideal situation, what kind of situation is ideal when you're trying to break up with someone - especially someone you still love and don't really *want* to break up with? However, it allowed me to talk to her in person within a finite time frame since she had another plane to catch.

Although one might expect, given the circumstances, that she would be understanding despite her disappointment - that was not the case. I tried to explain that although my feelings for her had not changed, I just could not manage the emotions that came with the idea of my dad dying feeling the way he did about me. Again, it was a classic, legitimate, "It's not you, it's me" situation, but she just could not accept it. In fact, she was so upset that by the time she left, I had agreed to try to continue to make things work, only to end up breaking up with her over the phone weeks later, anyway.

As you can probably imagine, that did not go any better. In fact, a couple weeks later I received a package from her that was a larger box than necessary to hold the contents. As a result, the box was all beaten up and disfigured when it arrived. Inside was every memento she could have ever thought to save from our year and a half relationship. Every card and letter I'd ever sent to her. Every photo she had of us. Even the ticket stubs from the movies we'd seen together. I couldn't think of one thing she may have possibly kept that had to do with us. My heart was broken. Not only because I knew there was no point of return with her, but especially because it was evident that she was incredibly hurt by my inability to stand up for our relationship. It would take 20 years for me to come to understand that my heart was also broken by my inability to stand up for myself. I didn't respond to the package. I didn't feel worthy of a conversation with her and even if I did, there was nothing I could say. I felt terrible that she was so hurt about it, but I still could not bring myself to make a different choice, so what really was there to talk about?

A few weeks later, my mom called to question me about an arrangement of flowers that had been delivered to their house. The card attached was a "Get Well Soon" card signed simply as "Tawnny." I explained to my mom that I had ended things with her and that she had not taken it well. I was sure that Tawnny sent the flowers with the intention of causing drama with my family, and I apologized if it had upset Dad. Sounding relieved, my mom assured me that it was fine and promptly changed the subject.

About a week after that call, I was sitting in the living room of my off-campus apartment with a couple of my roommates when I received an emotional call from my mom.

My dad had been admitted to the hospital, yet again. My mom was particularly upset and eventually handed the phone over to Jen Duman, who was a friend of the family. There have been *so* many Jennifers in my life. This one was a year younger than me. I'd grown up with her and her older brother.

"Jen, what is going on? Is he going to be okay? Do I need to come home?" I asked. At this point, I was beginning to get distraught. It was Wednesday and I had my dance company's concert performance that weekend. I was having a hard time understanding exactly what was going on with him and gauging whether this was just another trip to the hospital or a life or death situation that required my immediate presence.

"He's alright," Jen reassured me. "They're giving him as much pain medication as he wants, but he's okay right now."

Anyone who has had any experience with end of life care would have immediately recognized this information as a red flag, code for, "He's on his way out." But I didn't have that frame of reference. I was nineteen. All of my grandparents - the people we expect to lose first - were still living.

Feeling somewhat calmed by her words, I decided I would stay for my dance performances and head home immediately after Saturday's show. When my mom got back on the phone, she said that if he was feeling better on Saturday, she and my sister would still come up to see my show.

"No. I want you to stay with Dad. If he's going to be okay, I will stay and dance my shows and I will come home immediately after," I insisted.

"Okay," my mom replied.

"Please tell him I love him and I will be home to see him as soon as the show is over," I said before saying goodbye to my mom for the night.

Soon, I would come to regret the decision to stay and dance my show. It would take years, but eventually I would look back on this conversation and realize the huge lack of communication between me and my mom. We were both deep in our own denial which prevented me from asking if my dad was going to die and her from telling me he was. I didn't want to know the truth and she didn't want it to be the truth, but on some level, I believe we both knew what was happening.

Early Saturday morning before the sun had risen, I woke to the ringing of my phone. It always makes my heart race when I'm woken abruptly, but this was a whole other situation.

"Hello?" I answered.

"Jennifer? It's Stacie." I heard from the other end. "The hospital just called your mom and said that your dad is having labored breathing and that she should come over right away. We're going to come and get you from school." At this point, my mind was still asleep, although my heart and the rest of my body seemed to be wide awake. Too slow to be able to process all the things at once, I reacted to the last thing she said.

"I'm two and a half hours away! You can't come and get me. I will drive home," I tell her, my heart racing and sensing that time is of the essence.

"I really don't want you to drive yourself. Is there someone who can drive you home?" Stacie asked, sounding concerned.

"My truck is a stick and none of my roommates can drive it."

"Well, can someone at least ride along with you?"

"Uh, yes...yes, probably. Hold on, I'll go see."

I put the phone down on the bed and headed to my roommate's room. I knocked softly on the door and then let myself in.

"Angelic!" I loudly whispered as I approached her bedside, trying not to wake the rest of the apartment. She woke as dazed and confused and startled as I had.

"My aunt is on the phone. It's my dad. I need to go home right now. Can you please come with me?" At this point, I began to lose my composure and the reality of what was happening starts to set in.

Without missing a beat, Angelic says, "Yes. Yes, let me just call work and let them know I'm not coming."

"Thank you!" I tearfully whispered as I headed back to my bedroom to let my aunt Stacie know that Angelic will be coming with me.

"My roommate is coming with me. We're leaving as soon as I get my clothes on," I tell her.

"Ok, please be careful, Jennifer."

"I will." We hung up and Angelic and I got on the road moments later.

Once I was more awake, I found myself trying to figure out where Stacie was when she called me. Stacie was my dad's sister and had been like a big sister to me growing up. She and my Uncle Mitch lived eight hours away and no one had mentioned anything about them having come home to be with my dad. It caused me to wonder if they knew something I didn't for them to make that trip. As I made the two and a half hour drive, I prayed, "Please Dad, just hold on until I get there."

I knew my way around the hospital from having worked there for two years. I quickly and confidently took the north tower elevators directly to his unit, bypassing the main entrance and lobbies of the hospital and walked right into his room. As I neared his door, I noticed it was not completely closed, so I slowly pushed the door open and tried to enter the room quietly. I immediately made eye-contact with my Uncle Mitch who was standing against the wall opposite the door. As I made my way across the small, private room to my uncle, I looked in the direction of my dad. His eyes were wide open and his gaze was toward the window. I immediately looked away.

Hugging my uncle, the tears began to fall. Still not

wanting to let my dad see me cry about his illness, I whispered to Mitch, "Can he hear me?"

Confused, he whispered back, "What, honey?"

Pulling my head back from his shoulder a bit, I repeated myself, "Can he hear me?"

"Honey...he's gone," he replied. I felt my knees go out from under me as I collapsed into his arms, loudly sobbing.

Before I knew it my mom, who had been waiting for me in the third floor main lobby, was in the room and whisking me out of the room and down to the main lobby where the rest of my family was waiting. As she escorted me out, I had this feeling of bewilderment at the thought of never speaking to my dad again.

Between my sobbing I said to her, "I can't remember the last time I talked to him!"

As if she knew I was going to ask that question, without any hesitation, she immediately replied, "You talked to him Tuesday night."

My mind raced trying to recall the conversation. "I can't remember what we talked about!"

I sobbed without end while my mother began to relay back to me some of our conversation. Before I knew it, we were walking into the third floor lobby where literally all of my family were gathered. I felt on display as they watched me lose my shit over the same trauma they had already had at least two hours to process. I was so uncomfortable. I felt incredibly exposed and like I needed to compose myself in private.

Once I had calmed down a bit, my Aunt Stacie asked me if I would like to spend some time with my dad before they took his body away. I didn't know if I wanted to, but felt like I should. Stacie walked me back to the room where she left me to be alone with him. I had her move the chair to the other side of his bed because I could not handle looking into his lifeless eyes. Even in death, I could not bring myself to say anything about what had happened between us over the last year. I cried and whispered "I'm sorry," but did not speak what I was sorry for. I didn't know what I was sorry for at that point. I wasn't sorry for loving Tawnny. Maybe I was sorry for disappointing him. Maybe I was sorry for disappointing myself. Too uncomfortable with the emotions of it, and worried that someone might come in or overhear my "conversation" with him, I quickly shifted my focus to what felt better.

He was supposed to have come to see my dance concert that night. I said to him, "I wish you could see me dance one last time." Immediately, I knew I would go back to campus that night and perform. I felt like he would be watching from Heaven and that would be my way of saying goodbye to him.

As I left my dad's hospital room, I pulled my mom aside.

"Did you tell him about the flowers?" I asked, hesitantly.

"Yes, I told him," she replied.

"You told him it was over?" I clarified.

"Yes."

"What did he say?" I asked.

"He said, 'Good. Throw those fucking things away,'" she said.

For whatever reason, that morning at the hospital, it was so important to me that he knew about this conversation before he passed away. Initially, I was upset that Tawnny sent those flowers to the house. However, later I would come to realize that what she had intended to be hurtful was a blessing in disguise. Had she not sent those flowers, I would not have had the conversation with my mom that the relationship was over. There was some sort of unexplainable comfort in knowing that my dad knew things were over between me and her, even if I wasn't sure I would never be in a relationship with another woman. Maybe it was about giving him some kind of peace that he hadn't failed as a father. Maybe it was about feeling like I hadn't given up the relationship with her for nothing. Maybe it was about feeling like I'd regained my dad's approval and him knowing I was still a kid he could die proud of. Maybe it was a combination of all of these. Ultimately, it brought me - and I like to think him - peace...and maybe that's all that matters.

CHAPTER NINE

Grace Embodied

There is nothing like the death of a loved one to make you realize that time doesn't stop for anyone or anything. After they came for my dad's body, we all began to think about what had to be done next. There were funeral arrangements to be made, decisions to be made about clothes he would be buried in, who would carry his casket, where he would be buried, who would preach his service, plots to be purchased, food to be ordered, photos to be gathered, and a million other details that immediately became the only thing happening in our lives. Initially, I thought this meant I would miss my dance concert that night. In fact, I'd already contacted one of my roommates who was in the show with me to let her know that I would not be there. However, having missed my dad's departure from his body, I felt like performing for him that night would be my way of saying goodbye to him and having some kind of closure.

"Is it weird that I feel like I want to go back up to campus and dance tonight?" I asked my mom through tears. I was worried that she or others might perceive my leaving my family the night that my dad passed away as insensitive.

"No, honey, that's not weird," my mom comforted.

"Would you be upset if I go? I just feel like he will be there and I would like to dance for him one last time. It just feels like my way of saying goodbye," I explained.

"No, I will not be upset. You do whatever you feel like you need to do," my mom assured me.

That morning, Jake, who was now living and working in Detroit, met me at the hospital. Once it was clear that there was nothing more to be done at the hospital, he followed me the less than two mile drive to my parents' house where we left my truck. After saying goodbye to my mom and my sister, he drove me back to Mount Pleasant for the dance concert. Emotionally exhausted, I slept most of the way.

When we arrived to my apartment in the early afternoon, it was quiet. Angelic, who had accompanied me to the hospital earlier that morning, had decided to take advantage of being in the Detroit area and spend the rest of the weekend with her family. My other roommates were either working or also away for the weekend. I had a few hours before I would need to report to the theater for the dance concert. For maybe the first time in my life, I felt a bit like a kid. I felt lost and exhausted and really didn't know what to do.

It was the first time I could remember really needing to be taken care of and Jake was truly Heaven-sent. He led me directly to my bed where he got in first and then invited me to curl up in his arms and let go. We both slept for a few hours before it was time to get up and shower and get ready for the show. When I got up to go to the bathroom to shower, I hesitated to leave the room.

"Are you okay?" Jake asked.

"Yeah...I just feel kind of afraid to be alone," I said as I stood in the hallway outside my bedroom. "I feel like I'm going to open my eyes or turn around and see my dad standing there."

He went ahead of me into the bathroom and turned on the shower for me. Standing in the doorway, he invited me into the bathroom. "I'll be right down the hall if you need me. I'll leave your door open so I can hear if you call for me," he said before closing me in the bathroom and returning to my room. I made it through my shower without any strange appearances from my dad. In a fog, I got dressed, gathered my things, and we headed to the theater.

Although I had communicated my father's passing to my roommate, who was in the company with me, and she had shared the information with the director of the company, no one else knew. This allowed for me to keep that information to myself until I was ready to share it and to control my emotions that would have surely come up with every acknowledgement of his passing.

I had three dance numbers that night. Jake was watching from the audience. The first two performances felt like I was just going through the motions. That must have been evident to Jake because as I stood in the darkness of the wings watching a haunting duet while waiting to go on for my final number, I suddenly felt his comforting arms wrap around me from behind. Realizing that he had startled me at first, he whispered, soothingly, "It's me. It's just me," directly into my left ear. He held me in silence for a few moments and feeling his body breathe as he held mine calmed me and helped me feel centered.

"Close your eyes," he said, still holding me from behind. As we stood in the darkness, he continued to whisper in my ear. "You came tonight to dance for your dad. Let go of your thoughts. Let your heart lead you and shine like you always do. He's here to see you."

At the sound of applause from the audience, I opened my eyes to see the dancers from the previous number exiting the stage and the lights going down. It was showtime for me. Jake gave me a final soft squeeze and a kiss on the cheek before releasing me from his embrace. I took the stage with my group, took a deep breath and did my very best to let go and really let the piece dance me. It definitely felt different from the previous performances. When it was over, as the lights went down on us, I blew a kiss toward the sky as I said goodbye to my dad before exiting the stage.

The next few days were long and draining. We had visitation for my dad all day Sunday, all day Monday, and the funeral service was Tuesday morning. Having worked maintenance at the local hospital for his whole adult life, my dad got to know a lot of people in every part of the hospital. He also had many friends who still lived in the area and came to pay their respects even if they hadn't seen him in years. Then there were my mom's friends, my sister's friends, friends of my dad's family, my friends, my pom-pon coaches, even Girl Scout leaders from when I was a kid. It was so overwhelming to feel so much love from so many people that, even now as I write about it, I am overcome with gratitude.

For two full days, the funeral home was wall-to-wall people. There were times when it was difficult to even walk through the room. I found myself feeling like I was walking around in a dream. At one point, exhausted, I sat down on a couch at the back of the room and finally resigned to the philosophy, *if people want to talk to me, they'll come to me.*

I am convinced that it was by the Grace of God that Jake came into my life for the purpose of supporting me through this very difficult time. Despite not knowing my family well, he stayed at the funeral home throughout all of the visitation hours. In much the same manner that he had held space for me the weekend that I told him about Tawnny, he gave me space to visit with the endless stream of people who came through the door, yet made his presence felt in the event I needed him. In fact, most of the time, others wouldn't have even known he was there. He would quietly come and find me and check on me from time to time. Each time he would offer to get me anything I might need. Then he'd disappear again into one of the living room areas where I knew I could find him when I needed a break and someone to just be with me. He seemed to have such a clear understanding of exactly what I needed from him; even when I didn't know myself. I don't know many people who would spend that kind of time simply being present amongst strangers, making themselves available for when they are needed. He was literally God's hands and feet, being near me and holding me when I needed to be held. I'm so grateful that Spirit provided me with so much grace through Jake's love and support.

Jake and I continued to date for almost a year after my dad's passing. Although it became clear that we were in a more committed relationship, there was still not the kind of chemistry I had experienced in other relationships. Despite there being times when I seemed to feel it from him, he never uttered the words "I love you." I also sensed that even though there were times when I felt it, I should also avoid saying it. So, I did. It felt more like going through the motions in a relationship that I was supposed to be in based on other people's expectations, than a love that consumes the heart, mind, and soul and makes you feel alive all over. But it was comfortable and it was safe. Jake was an amazing guy by everyone's account. In my mind, I had no reason to break up with him. At that point I had yet to learn that the relationship not being what I wanted it to be was reason enough to end it. So, I stayed. Until I encountered the next person who made me feel alive.

CHAPTER TEN

The Second Coming

It was fall of 1997, about nine months after I lost my dad, when I met the next woman I would fall in love with. Incidentally, I also met my future husband, but it would take us fourteen years to figure that out. As the resident assistant for the floor, I connected with her before I even met her. Having grown up with the last name Miracle, her last name immediately caught my attention as I prepared to make door decorations for each person who would be moving onto our floor. Anointed with a name like "Best," it was almost as if the Universe was making sure I didn't miss her.

On move-in day, residents began arriving one by one at first and then the pace quickened as more and more of them filed in. I was an excited new resident assistant, so I fluttered around the floor, introducing myself to residents. I would be lying if I said I had a significant moment with her on that particular day, beyond my surprise that she was not at all what I anticipated based on her very girly first and middle name, Elizabeth Ainsley. I think I had envisioned a much more feminine, make-up wearing, sorority-rushing type of girl. Instead, I was met with a level of confidence, directness, and charm that I was unaccustomed to in my relationships with women - friendship or otherwise - and I wasn't sure I knew what to make of that.

Within the first few weeks of the semester, I somehow found myself in an awkward situation with Ainsley, as she preferred to be called. We were alone and she asked if she could kiss me. She was so forward and unapologetic. Despite the attraction that I felt when I was with her, I was also super uneasy about it. I sensed her boldness and the Leo in her that would have made it impossible to keep a romantic relationship between a student and her RA under wraps. She was dangerous and I was still reeling from the loss of the relationship with my dad and his subsequent passing, both of which at that time felt like they were the price I paid for the last relationship I'd been in with someone who was "off limits." I wasn't ready to play those high stakes again, this time risking my job, and therefore my room and board. In retrospect, it was probably the only thing that kept me from kissing her that night. Being the "responsible RA" that I was, I told her no, and gave her the line - which wasn't a line - about how I was not allowed to date my residents. Besides that, I still had a boyfriend.

A few days later, Ainsley's roommate, Kacie, came to me for support. Kacie's mom had found out about the relationship she had been having with her female best friend, Emma, earlier in the summer and had not been speaking to her since. While Kacie was no longer in that relationship, her mom was under the assumption that she still was, and gave her an ultimatum after dropping her off at college. Additionally, her mom had not told her dad about what was going on. There were some striking similarities between what Kacie was currently going through and what I had been through with my own family and we immediately bonded. Before I knew it, I realized that there were strong feelings developing between the two of us. However, there was also an understanding that those feelings could not be public. At the risk of losing my job, I broke up with Jake and immediately began seeing Kacie. Surprisingly, things were never awkward between me and Ainsley even though I was now dating her roommate right after I had told her that was against the rules. Ainsley ended up dating another woman on our floor and we all continued to be friends and spent lots of time together. It was, without a doubt, one of the best years of my life.

Kacie and I were together for about four and a half years. During that time, I graduated from college and returned to Central Michigan University as a professional staff member in August of 2000. Although Kacie was the second woman I had been in a relationship with, at some point, I felt it necessary to come out to my mom. Again. Especially considering that my mom knew that I had dated Jake for so long. While it seemed obvious and maybe even understood that Kacie and I were a couple, something in me felt it necessary to speak the words to my mom so that there was no misunderstanding. There was something exhausting about tiptoeing around the subject and worrying about my mom confronting me about it. I had gotten to the point that having a difficult conversation about it was more appealing than not having the conversation at all. Before I moved back to Mount Pleasant to start my job at CMU, I sat down with my mom.

"There's something I want to tell you," I said hesitantly.

"Okay," my mom replied.

I gave her some sort of rambling lead-in about how, "I know you're not necessarily going to be happy but I hope you will love me anyway, and I just really need to be honest," before finally saying, "Kacie and I are a couple."

"Did you think I didn't know?" my mom replied in a tone that was not anger, but also not genuine curiosity.

"Well, I guess not...I just felt like I needed to say it."

There was an awkward silence as I sat on the ottoman across from the couch my mom was sitting on in our quaint living room. The late summer sunlight was shining through the picture window behind her.

I still couldn't discern how she felt about it based on her response. It had been almost three years since my dad passed away and Kacie and I had been together for two of those. She had clearly had some time to process the idea, but it had never been spoken about again. Based on past experience I did not expect her overwhelming support. I also felt like I needed to understand how she felt about it. I needed to know what I was dealing with. Sensing that I was waiting for some kind of response, my mom finally broke the silence.

"Look. Do I like it? No. Would I change it if I could? Probably," she said looking me in the eye. "But life is too short to let that come between us."

I felt incredibly relieved by this response. While I hadn't anticipated a volatile reaction like I'd experienced the first time around, I also did not expect a response that seemed to be accepting. I would not have been surprised by a more "It's none of my business" type response, so her willingness to state that she did not want it to come between us meant a lot to me. Although we would disagree about many things in the years after my dad passed, I can say that my mom has always made good on not letting my sexual orientation be a thing that came between us.

CHAPTER ELEVEN
Finding My Light

I have always had this feeling or belief that I was going to somehow be famous. I didn't ever envision it being a situation of celebrity status, but I just had this anticipation of being prestigious for doing something "important" in the world. As a young person, I feel like I was much more ambitious and confident about it despite not even knowing what *it* was. Still, even as I write this book, an anticipation of being seen by those who will benefit from the Light I am shining in the world hangs in the ethers and summons me to action toward my goals.

I also grew up with this idea that if I did everything right and everything that was expected of me, I would be a success, and that would make me important. I lived for the approval of adults and was a natural overachiever. I was raised with the idea that you go to school, you get a degree which will get you a good paying job, you get married, have kids, and live happily ever after. Everyone was going to grow up to be a doctor, a lawyer, or member of some other highly-respected, and of course, highly-paid profession. The concept of a career being one's "calling" was completely foreign to me. Even the expression "I think you missed your calling," was only used in jest when someone was doing something silly that was clearly not career-worthy or respectable. So, when I found my Calling I don't think I even recognized it as such at the time. I just knew that I felt a passion ignite inside me and that I had to follow it.

In August of 2000, nearly four years after my dad passed away, I found myself back at my alma mater for my first full-time, salaried position; my first "real job" as I would come to think of it - as if jobs that didn't require a degree were somehow not real. It was a position I had never envisioned myself in. I was an assistant director at the student activity center on campus. I knew nothing about health or fitness, but I was an alum with a degree in recreation which helped get my foot in the door. My internship at Disney World and experience with guest service would be what set me apart from other candidates. As it turned out, Disney World had impacted my life in ways far beyond my imagination. When I started this new position, I made a promise to myself that I was going to be honest about who I was and who I loved. I would not hide for anyone anymore, and being a couple hours away from my mom gave me the freedom to truly live life authentically.

I had been in my position for about two years when I found myself feeling completely apathetic about life. I was single for the first time since 7th grade and living alone in my own apartment for the first time. I had a full-time, salaried, professional position, and was totally out about my sexuality.

Despite being settled, I felt like I was simply going through the motions. Things had been so different since my dad passed away. My mom, my sister, and I had all dealt with the grief so differently, and really, in isolation from one another. I returned to campus the week after the funeral to finish the semester, leaving my grieving fifteen year-old sister home with my also grieving mother. I think it was a rough ride for both of them for a while and eventually, when she turned 18, my sister headed south to live with my aunt and uncle. At the time, it seemed like the right thing to do; the thing my dad would want me to do. He and my grandpa had always stressed how important an education was. However, six years later, I found myself feeling disconnected, both physically and emotionally from my mom and my sister. I felt alone and found myself pondering the purpose of life. I had a moment in the shower one day as I willed myself to finally get up and get ready for work in which I wondered, *what's the fucking point?* Fortunately, my immediate next thought was the realization, *that's fucked up. You need to talk to someone.* I made an appointment to see the first therapist I had seen since my undergraduate experience.

Interestingly, it was just a few months later when a former student employee who had also become a friend encouraged me to get involved with the Office of Gay & Lesbian Programs on campus. He had left the position with our department to work in that office and was now in charge of coordinating speaker panels of people who would go into classrooms and share their coming out stories. Knowing me personally and how things had gone for me with my dad, he really felt that my story would be a powerful one to share with people. While I had made the promise to myself to be honest about who I was, I also didn't know how I felt about telling my coming out story to a roomful of strangers. My friend persuaded me to at least come to the training and to make a decision after I had a better understanding of what it was all about. After attending the training, I agreed to give the speaker panels a try.

I felt a little anxious about taking this step because it felt like something that couldn't be undone. I fully understood that once I shared my story, it would basically be public knowledge. What I couldn't be sure of is what the consequences of doing so may be. One of the very people who raised me and who was supposed to love me unconditionally, rejected me based solely on this characteristic alone. What might perfect strangers do to me?

When the day finally arrived, I stood outside of the classroom where we'd be speaking. As I watched people continuously filing into the room I saw one of the students I supervised. My heart started racing. Somehow, it had never occurred to me until that very moment that I might someday find myself sitting on a panel in a room that one of my students was in. As I spoke this realization out loud, I was given the opportunity to opt out of the panel at the last minute, but chose to tell my story and hope for the best.

That is the earliest memory I have of the start of my journey to my Calling. While I had sat on a few other panels before this one, as far as I knew, I had been speaking to strangers to which my sexual orientation was completely inconsequential. Now there was at least one person in the room who, to this point, had only seen me through a professional lens. That student was going to have access to a facet of my life that had only been seen by very select people. I had no idea how this person would manage this additional information. It was completely out of my hands. I found comfort in knowing that I worked in a department that was completely supportive of my involvement with this program and tried to embrace the opportunity that might be presented to further educate students in our department should it stir up questions or dialogue.

The format of the panels was that each person was given five minutes to share their coming out story and then the floor was open for questions. This was a great format because no one can tell their whole story in detail in just five minutes, so it often created a lot of questions and engagement. It also provided an opportunity for discussion about a topic that was typically off limits, especially at that time in our country. Although initially I had been anxious about putting myself in a position to potentially be judged or challenged by individuals in the audience - especially given the way my own father had treated me - I quickly became hooked on the reward of seeing a light go on for someone when they were able to ask a question and receive an answer that broadened their perspective or shifted their paradigm. I came to love this experience and took the opportunity to sit on a speaker panel as often as my schedule would allow.

CHAPTER TWELVE
Strike Two

In the summer of 2004, I was fresh out of my first live-in relationship, which had been with a woman, when I crossed paths again with Ainsley Best. Being the serial monogamist that I was, I promptly explored Yahoo personals for a possible new relationship when I came across my old friend from Troutman Hall. We immediately made plans to meet and catch up. Although it was never intended to be a date, it ended up being the epitome of a date. We had dinner, got ice cream, and even played putt-putt golf. Totally a date.

I was struck by Ainsley's masculine presence when we met in person, despite having seen her photo online. It was more than just a short haircut and masculine clothes. There was a familiar energy about her that had always felt intensely grounded and confident. I had been intimidated by this energy when we had that first moment in 1997, where she propositioned me for a kiss in my dorm room and I turned her down. But now, seven years later, that same energy seemed to emanate from her in a way that was super attractive. It was almost as if her outer appearance was more aligned with her inner essence and that somehow magnified this energy. At the same time, there was a dissonance for me between feeling attracted to her, and being a little put off by a woman looking and feeling so much like a man. Turns out I was transphobic before I even knew what transphobia was - and before she knew she was transgender.

It felt good to reconnect after having lost touch since we'd lived in Troutman Hall. We ended up making plans a few weeks later to get together again, this time at my house. At this point, I was working for my alma mater. She had left college during her second year and hadn't been back to campus, so she welcomed the opportunity to come back to Mount Pleasant. Although I didn't remember this detail until I was reminded of it another seven years later, I had invited Ainsley over to "have some beers and watch a movie"- clearly the equivalent of today's "Netflix and chill." So, here we were again and I had clearly opened the door for another proposition. That door was swiftly closed when, later in the evening, my roommate came home and brought a group of our friends with her. Immediately, all of my attention and energy was drawn to one of the women in the group and any connection Ainsley and I had was completely shut down. It was late by the time everyone left and I invited Ainsley to sleep on the couch which I would later learn was received as a bit of a sucker punch. She laid on the couch until she figured I was asleep and then slipped out the front door.

Neither of us has any recollection of how we came back from that awkward situation. However, later that fall, we hung out together again in Mount Pleasant at a bar off campus.

This time a mutual friend who had also lived on our floor in Troutman Hall joined us along with the woman who had usurped all of my attention the night we were supposed to old-school Netflix and chill, as we were now dating. Ainsley had also moved on and was dating a woman who, interestingly, shared the same birthdate as me. It was a fun night out with old and new friends, but would be the last time we saw each other for another seven years.

CHAPTER THIRTEEN
Finding My Calling

My involvement with the Office of Gay & Lesbian Programs quickly snowballed from sitting on panels, to facilitating them, to facilitating training of new volunteers for the panels. I eventually led the Association of Lesbian and Gay Faculty and Staff and had my hand in just about anything that was happening on campus that had to do with "gay stuff" as well as other diversity and inclusion. In 2005, when we had our first out transgender student coming to campus, I was also included in the day-long in-service that was being provided for the purpose of preparing our student affairs staff to best serve her. It was this in-service experience in which I unwittingly discovered my Calling.

The in-service was led by the director of the LGBT Resource Center at Michigan State University and a few students who were transgender. It blew my mind. At that point, I don't know if I even knew what transgender meant. So, it had certainly never occurred to me to think about what it might be like to live in the world as a transgender person. While the training covered the basics, it also got into the mundane parts of life and really gave us a look into how difficult it was, especially at that time, to live authentically as a transgender individual. Of course, there was a conversation about bathrooms. Today this is a conversation that we're having at the national level, but 15 years ago, the concept of having to deliberate about which bathroom to use completely eluded most people, myself included.

Although we talked about a wide range of things that day, I think the discussion that may have had the most impact on me was about the process of dating and navigating relationships. As if meeting the right person to spend your life with isn't complicated enough, my eyes were opened to how terrifying the process could be for a person who is transgender. I thought, *Man! I thought it was tough being a lesbian!* There were all kinds of questions about if and when to disclose one's transgender identity. The thought of having to negotiate when, if, even *how* to be one's authentic self just felt like way too much for anyone to have to bear. I felt overwhelmed and compelled to action. So much so, that at the end of the training day I approached the man who was leading the in-service and said, "I want to do what you do. I have a bachelor's degree. I'm sure I need a master's degree. I have no idea in what. How do I do what you do?"

I left that training with my head still spinning and couldn't wait to get home and share all that I had learned with my current girlfriend. It was one of those moments where I talked endlessly and she listened intently. As I shared with her the various struggles and everyday obstacles that transgender people deal with, my eyes began to well up with tears - the same tears that I would later recognize as Validation Tears. As I was passionately telling her about all I had learned she asked me, "Honey, are you going to cry?" That recognition of my passion released the floodgates as I replied, "Someone has to do this work!" and I knew it had to be me. So began my journey to earn my master's degree so that I could become the director of an LGBT Resource Center.

FINDING A CHURCH

CHAPTER FOURTEEN

Validation Tears

The first time I connected with Spirit it was purely on Their terms. It was a snowy, late December evening in 2005 and there was a Christmas concert at one of the local churches downtown. I had been to the show the previous year to see one of my co-workers sing in the choir. I had been impressed with the contemporary music and really enjoyed it. I guess that's how this year's event had ended up on my radar. I had seen signs for it and knew that I wanted to go again.

I tried to find someone to go with me a few days before the show, but was having no luck. Apparently, this church had a reputation for being somewhat of a cult. It was one of those new, hip churches with live bands and all kinds of cutting-edge media that occupied an old downtown theater. They were totally targeting the younger, college-student crowd even with its name - The Young Church. All that being said, it also had some crazy conservative values. I knew of some couples who attended the church who were not even allowed to kiss each other before marriage. Based on that knowledge alone, my sense was that it most certainly would not be welcoming to anyone who had even thought about kissing someone of the same sex. Since most of my friends at the time were women who liked to kiss other women or men who liked to kiss men, none of them were feeling too excited about venturing into any church, much less this one - even if it was only for a Christmas concert...my girlfriend included.

When the evening of the show arrived, I was left with the options of either going alone or not at all. Although it was out of character for me, I felt compelled to go alone. Not only that, but I walked there. In December. In Michigan. Who was I?? Granted, it was only a few blocks away, but at that point in my life I had not developed an awareness of the power of the connection to nature - and certainly not in winter weather. At any rate, I walked downtown and headed into the old theater and found a seat toward the back of the house, stage right.

I chose a row that was mostly empty and left plenty of seats between myself and the next person. It was uncomfortable enough being alone, so I didn't want to be sitting close to strangers, too. The show began with very traditional Christmas songs, "Silent Night," "It Came Upon a Midnight Clear," "We Three Kings," etc. Certainly nothing new, yet by the third carol I found myself moved to tears. There I was alone in the dark theater, with perfect strangers just a few feet away, and I could not stop the tears from falling. It was the oddest feeling. I could not identify the source of the tears. I wouldn't say I felt sad or happy, just inexplicably emotional. And I remained so throughout the *entire* hour-long show. In fact, when the show was over and the lights came up, I still could not stop the tears. Feeling the heat from my tears on my face and knowing that I get blotchy when I cry, I did my best to wipe them away and look presentable

As we all filed out of the nearly full church theater into the lobby that was exponentially smaller, I was suddenly shoulder to shoulder with what felt like half of Mount Pleasant and my tears continued to fall. As I moved through the crowd, I made eye contact with a student I knew who worked at the campus recreation center. I could see that she was serving as an usher. I knew her pretty well. In fact, I used to supervise her, so she also knew me more personally. I knew that she was a member of this "cult" church, and she knew that I was a lesbian and we were both totally okay with this situation. As the sea of people moved me toward the brisk, snowy night, our paths crossed and she gave me a hug. Unable to miss my streaming tears, she understandably asked if I was okay, to which I responded with an affirmative nod accompanied by an expression that hinted at another story I wasn't ready to tell.

I wandered out onto the sidewalk and headed in the direction of my apartment. The night air felt cold on my face which was warm and wet with tears. There were great big fluffy snowflakes falling and for the first time, I was in awe of the beauty of snow. It had been snowing for the better part of the day and everywhere I looked there was a gorgeous glistening light reflecting back at me. Although I was walking downtown, there was a hush in the air. It was almost as if I could hear the fresh snow falling. The tears continued to flow as I walked the few blocks home and still I can't explain the emotion, just that it wasn't sadness...and that it was very real.

When I returned to my apartment, I felt compelled to pick up my girlfriend's Bible. This might make it sound like Jen - yes, my girlfriend's name was also Jennifer - was religious, but that was not the case as far as I knew. It was a Bible her grandmother had given her, likely in hopes that she might become religious someday. At any rate, I opened it and began to read. At that point in my life, I'd never read the Bible, other than a few verses in the handful of Sunday school classes I had attended as a kid. I didn't get far before her version of the Bible started listing all of the names of all the generations and I was completely uninspired. However, I was also undeterred. It was about that time that she arrived home from work. I tried to explain to her the emotion of my experience and why I was reading the Bible. Although I tend to be an exceptional communicator, I found myself struggling to express to her what had gone on for me. I finally asked if she would go back to the show with me the next night. Although it was clear she didn't really understand the "magic" I had experienced, she graciously agreed to go.

The next morning, I woke up humming a song for the first and only time in my life. I didn't even realized I was humming it at first. It was like this subconscious thing...until it wasn't. I had a moment of realization when I suddenly recognized that I was humming a song that I'd never heard before seeing the show. It was called "My Heart, Your Home," and they introduced it as a prayer for those who were feeling far from God to ask Him to come into their heart and make it His home. I didn't remember the words or that it had even been introduced as a prayer but could not stop humming the chorus over and over and over. "*Come and make my heart your home, come and be everything I am and all I know. Search me through and through, til my heart becomes a home for you.*" It was like an affirmation that this experience I had had was not to be forgotten.

As promised, Jen accompanied me to the show that evening. This time I chose seats stage left and a little closer to the front. I didn't worry so much about our proximity to other people. Although the show certainly did not have the same effect on her as it had on me the night before, about halfway through, I was once again in tears. Still, I could not identify or explain the emotion, and again, I could not stop the tears.

On our way out of the theater, we purchased a CD of the show that I would listen to repeatedly for months to come. The first time I listened to it, I discovered a hidden track at the end - a song that had not been included in the show - that completely blew me away and gave me a new appreciation and understanding for what had happened that weekend that drew me to that show in the first place. Sadly, I have since lost that CD and cannot remember the melody or the lyrics of that song. I do, however, still remember the notion that it had been written just for me.

It described the feeling so many of us have experienced of loneliness and desperation of seeking something more, something larger than ourselves. There was specifically a lyric, that I'm sure must be referenced in Scripture somewhere, that mentioned some kind of gift that God places in each of our hearts that draws us back to Him. A piece of God in each of us that makes it impossible for us to ever be separated from our Creator - like some kind of homing device that cannot be disarmed or overridden by anything we think, say, or do, no matter how terrible, sinful, or unworthy we might think we are. It was as if this song had given an explanation to this powerful inclination I had to go to that Christmas show at that particular church, despite all the reasons not to...and it brought the same mysterious tears that I experienced the night before.

Although this was the first time I had experienced these tears, it would certainly not be the last. They would ultimately show up time and time again during church services in which the message being preached felt like it was specifically for me. They would show up during the first church service I attended with my future husband, and he would experience them, too. In retrospect, they had made an appearance as I passionately explained to my girlfriend all that I had learned during the in-service about serving transgender students. The tears showed up to communicate to me that I had found my

Calling; I was on the right path. I even remember being a young girl at one of the sporadic church services we would randomly attend and experiencing these tears - which the adults interpreted as me "feeling the Holy Spirit," but I was too young to really understand what that meant.

In fact, I've since come to recognize the indescribable emotions and tears as God's way of communicating with me directly, of letting me know that what I'm hearing, learning, understanding, knowing - even sometimes saying - is Divine and can be trusted. I've learned that because we all are unique creatures, we all have different ways in which we hear God's voice in our lives. God will use whatever means necessary to connect with us, if we just listen and pay attention. For some people, it comes in the form of a literal voice, for some it may be goosebumps, for others it is the presence of a particular animal or other meaningful symbol or synchronicity. Some can best describe it simply as a "knowing." Ultimately, it's a feeling that you cannot articulate. I could not articulate the emotion that brought my tears that night, but their wisdom was indisputably Divine.

I now affectionately refer to this method of discernment as "Validation Tears," and understanding it has allowed me to become much more comfortable with the emotion and the tears. It has also provided me with guidance and affirmation of life experiences, career choices, creative process, and just knowing that God is always with me. I know now that I will always have everything I need because everything I need is inside of me.

After this first conscious experience with God, I followed up with the friend who had hugged me in the lobby on my way out that night. I explained to her the connection I had felt with God for the first time in that space. I also explained to her that I'd heard some pretty problematic things about the church and their conservative values. Because she was also a student worker at the recreation center at the university where I worked, she was aware that I was a very out and visible staff member on campus. I asked her if she could tell me more about her experiences with the church and its beliefs about homosexuality.

She explained to me that they basically took the approach of "love the sinner, hate the sin." She used an analogy that has been used by countless conservative Christians that equates homosexuality to alcoholism. The implication is that, in both situations, one has a choice to engage in the activity. While they are not wrong about the notion of having a choice in whether to *engage* in sexual relationships or whether to have a drink of alcohol, this belief dismisses the fact that there is an innate aspect to sexual orientation that does not apply to drinking alcohol or other "bad habits." One is not born with a desire to drink alcohol. We all, however, are born with an innate desire to be connected with people in various ways, including ways that are sexual. Reaching the conclusion that this church was not going to be a safe place for me to be my authentic self, and unwilling to go back in the closet on any level, I let go of the possibility of this being a place for me to worship. However, I became more motivated to find a place where I could safely feel that Divine connection again. I had gotten a taste of it and sensed that there was so much more to experience.

CHAPTER FIFTEEN
Divine Providence

After declaring my dream of becoming the director of
an LGBT Resource Center, I immediately enrolled in a
graduate program and spent the next three years taking
classes while also working my full-time position and
continuing to be engaged in on-campus efforts to raise
awareness and increase education about gender and sexuality.
In the meantime, my girlfriend of nearly four years had
accepted a two-year graduate assistantship in Savannah,
Georgia. So, in the spring of 2008, I began searching for
student affairs jobs in Georgia with the hope of finding
something at least in the same state and ideally working with
LGBT students.

This seemed like a stretch considering I was trying to
move to the Bible Belt. However, one day the director
position at The University of Georgia showed up in my inbox
and I eagerly applied for the position. A few months passed
with no word on the status of the position. In the meantime,
my girlfriend had returned home from a year-long internship
and shortly after that our relationship ended. At that point,
still having one class left to finish as well as my own
internship experience in order to earn my master's degree, I

decided that the only job I would leave my current one for would be one working with LGBT students.

It was late July when I saw an email come through my inbox announcing that the director position at UGA had been reposted. They had failed the initial search and were still looking for the right candidate. I shared this information with my best friend, Jon, who was also in my program, and like me, had been advised by our faculty to follow up with all prospective employers. He reminded me of this advice and encouraged me to reach out and inquire about the status of my application. I argued that they clearly were not interested in me given that they had reposted the position. Still, Jon urged me to follow up anyway, and thank God I took his advice.

I replied to the message announcing the reposting of the position, mentioning that I had applied for the job during the initial search and was curious about the status of my application. I received a quick reply asking me if I would forward my resume and cover letter again. I obliged and received a phone call the next day from the woman who would eventually become my next supervisor. She was very direct and said, "I don't know what happened to your materials the first time around, but I never saw them. That's really neither here nor there at this point. We're moving very quickly with this search. Would you be interested in doing a phone interview with us?" This sounded promising already. I said, "Yes, I'd love to!" and we set an appointment for a phone interview the next afternoon.

If you have ever been through a phone interview I'm sure you will likely agree that, generally, they suck. You can't see anyone so you can't read people's faces or body language as you give responses to their questions. Additionally, because there are typically multiple people on the other end of the call, it's difficult to know who is speaking and it can be easy to talk at the same time which just makes it awkward. Miraculously, this was not my experience on this phone interview. In fact, the thirty minutes that were scheduled turned into a 45-minute interview and by the time we hung up, I felt really good about the possibility of moving forward in the process. Sure enough, I got a call back that afternoon inviting me to campus the following week. I had four days to find a suit and put together a 30-minute presentation about the role of an LGBT Resource Center at a flagship institution in the South...what?!

After a whirlwind of shopping for a business suit for a short girl and creating a presentation that was my best guess at what doing gender and sexuality work looked like in the Bible Belt, I was in for another whirlwind as I made my way to sunny - and sultry - Athens, GA for my on-campus interview. I had come to the conclusion that a black, skirted suit with a hot pink shirt was most fitting for the occasion and my personality. It communicated the understanding of the significance of the position and the university, while still expressing my individualized style. It was an incredibly long thirty-six hours. I experienced travel snafus on the way which forced me to have to drive myself the hour and fifteen minutes from the airport and back as opposed to being shuttled. The interview day itself was packed with back to back meetings from 9am until 4pm with everyone from a group of the students I'd be working with to the Vice President of Student Affairs. It was an exhausting day, but lunch helped to ease the stress a bit. My future supervisor ordered a single dessert to share with me and a co-worker and I began to feel like I was already part of the team.

By the time I arrived at my final meeting of the day, which was with the Vice President of Student Affairs, I was so spent that I was beginning to feel delirious. At some point, I wasn't even sure what he had just said because my mind was a swirl of activity. Immediately following that meeting, I was whisked away to my hotel where my rental car was parked and had to make my way back to the Atlanta airport. I talked briefly with Jon as I made my way out of Athens.

"Well!?!" He asked, excitedly. "How did it go??"

Having just sat down by myself for the first time in about eight hours, I started to process all that had happened. I felt completely overwhelmed and did not even know where to begin to tell him about the experience.

"Honestly, I can't even talk about it right now," I replied, exhausted.

Familiar with the intensity of an on-campus interview, Jon was understanding and assured me he was sure I did fabulous before letting me off the phone to focus on my drive. As soon as we hung up, I took a deep breath and settled into the fact that it was finally over. They had stressed that they were "moving quickly" with this search and so I anticipated I should hear something the next day. As I drove, I thought to myself with excitement, *I think I got this job!* And then almost immediately, I thought, *Oh my god. I think I got this job,* as a sense of dread and fear washed over me. *What if I got this job?!?*

In that moment, it occurred to me that I really had not seriously thought beyond the interview. I had officially jumped through all the hoops and achieved the dream I set out to achieve a few years earlier. Now, for the first time, I was being faced with what that might actually look like, and I was equal parts terrified and excited. In that moment, I realized everything I knew might be about to change.

CHAPTER SIXTEEN
Well Played, JC

It was official.

I had exactly three weeks to give my notice to my current job as well as to my apartment leasing office. I then needed to pack my things, find a place to live, and move to Athens, Georgia where I would begin my dream job as the Director of the LGBT Resource Center at the University of Georgia. I was scheduled to start on August 22nd, the first Friday of fall classes. In the meantime, I was also required to attend my new department's fall retreat a week before I began work. This made the transition much more complicated than I would have liked. Ultimately, it meant flying down on Thursday for the Friday retreat and flying back on Saturday. Then, that Monday, I would begin my road trip with all my things - including both my cats - in order to be settled and ready to start work on the following Friday.

While it would have been nice to have been completely moved to Georgia prior to the department retreat, doing so would have prevented me from giving even two weeks notice in a culture where giving thirty days notice seemed to be the norm. I was already feeling guilty about announcing my departure just weeks before fall semester began. My department had been so supportive of my journey and pursuing my dreams that I really didn't want to leave them hanging by jumping ship. There was also the small detail that I needed to find a place to live! In addition to doing a lot in a very short period of time, I was still in shock that I had set a goal, gone after it, and now my dream was coming true.

Even while all of this was going on, I was still motivated to explore the opportunities for connecting with God so I had begun going to a local, non-denominational community church. It was easily the largest congregation in the small college town of Mount Pleasant. Fitting into the megachurch category, they had parking attendants that helped to direct traffic flow, managing the mass exit of vehicles after the early service before the mass entrance of vehicles for the next service. Once you got to the entrance, there was a team of volunteer greeters and ushers directing people-traffic through the lobby toward the large sanctuary.

There was even an opportunity to hang up your coat and grab some coffee before heading in to find your seat. The sanctuary felt more like a theatre with multiple entry doors, an elevated stage with two large projection screens on either side, and mood lighting. They had impressive live music and state-of-the-art video messages much like the experience at The Young Church. At the door, you received a program for the day's service which also included lots of information about various ministries you could become involved in. It felt much more like a community. Despite the size of the congregation, people seemed to know each other.

This became a comfortable place for me to continue to practice attending church regularly without the pressure of anyone really expecting me to be there. I found that, due to the size of the congregation, I was able to attend while pretty much flying under the radar. This was important to me because I wasn't completely sold on the whole church thing yet. I just knew that I wanted to feel that same connection I had felt at that Christmas concert and church was the only way I knew of, at that point in my life, to look for it. I appreciated being able to do that without having to worry about other people's perceptions or judgments about what I knew or didn't know about God or the Bible.

The Sunday after I accepted the position at UGA, I attended service. A night owl by nature, I've never been an early riser and so I snuck in a few minutes into the service as was customary for me.

The church was trying out a new "cafe style" set-up for the summer where they had rows of chairs across the center part of the sanctuary and then large round tables that each sat about eight people on the outer aisles. The idea was that people could grab some coffee in the lobby on the way in and feel like they were at some kind of open mic event. Given that this was already the "late" service and I was also running later than all the other night owls, it was challenging to find a seat, especially since it was dark like a theater might be. I made my way to the far side of the sanctuary and eventually found a seat at one of the round tables situated about halfway toward the front of the room.

As I was trying to get seated as inconspicuously as possible, the pastor started introducing a special visitor. He briefly mentioned the outstanding work this man was doing and then invited him to the stage to share his story with the congregation. My heart dropped into my stomach when the pastor introduced him as Fred Phelps and the congregation applauded, welcoming him to the stage. While I realize now that there are perhaps hundreds - maybe thousands? - of men named "Fred Phelps" in the world, at that moment in time and in the context of my life, there was only one Fred Phelps, and he was the notorious leader of the Westboro Baptist Church in Topeka, Kansas. You know, the "God Hates Fags" guy? If you don't know, consider yourself lucky. To be fair, that was about all I really knew about him at the time. Nonetheless, the idea that he was about to take the stage at this church struck such fear in me that I almost made a beeline for the door. I looked around the room and tried to calculate my quickest escape. And then, as I sat there, freaking out, tension building in my legs as I contemplated springing to my feet and making a run for it, a calmness came over me.

I received this message of, *Jennifer. You just accepted the position of director of the LGBT Resource Center at the University of Georgia, and Topeka, Kansas is a whole lot closer to Georgia than it is to Michigan. So you need to sit here and figure out what you're going to do.* It was not an audible message, just a kind of knowing or understanding - but the words were clear. I remember it vividly. With that, I became aware of my quickened breathing and racing heart and focused on slowing that all down and tuning in to what was happening on the stage.

By this time, this Fred Phelps guy had made his way to the stage and was humbly sharing about the work he and his missionary group had been doing with regard to translating The Bible to various different languages in a litany of other countries and distributing them throughout the world. He went on and on and eventually left the stage without even one mention of "homosexuals" and the damage they were doing to the fabric of our society. I was both relieved and perplexed.

As he made his way back to his seat, the pastor returned and introduced the theme of the preaching series which was "Things That Amaze Me." He explained that the morning's sermon was going to be based on the story of David and Goliath. If you're familiar with the story of David & Goliath at all, you probably know that it's a bit of an underdog story in that this small, young boy David overcomes the giant, monstrous enemy, Goliath. What I did not know of this story until it was shared at this service, is that despite being the youngest and weakest of eight brothers, David was chosen by God to be the next king of Israel prior to the battle with Goliath. The pastor stressed that no one expected it to be David, including David himself. No one even necessarily had any faith in David as a leader, but God had chosen David.

Samuel, whom God had sent to find the next king, anointed him with the power of the Lord. Ultimately, it was David's great faith in God that allowed him to slay Goliath.

As I learned this added detail, along came my Validation Tears. I received the message loud and clear from God. Like David, God had chosen me to do this work. I suddenly knew that despite my own doubts about my ability to do the job I'd just accepted, and any fears that I might have about my own Goliaths, God had chosen me and would see to it that I was successful. I left the service that day feeling amazed; like God had spoken directly to me through the message that was delivered. I felt empowered and reassured that I could really do this job.

When I got home, I Googled Fred Phelps. Although he had a notorious reputation that clearly preceded him, I had no idea what the guy actually looked like. Much to my chagrin the guy named Fred Phelps who had spoken at church earlier in the day was *not* the same Fred Phelps who led the Westboro Baptist Church. God sure did get my attention with him at the beginning of service, though. Well played, JC. Well. Played.

CHAPTER SEVENTEEN
My First Answered Prayer

Once I had signed the offer letter accepting the position at Georgia, my supervisor sent out an announcement to the university community sharing the good news that they had finally filled the position and welcoming me to Georgia. Almost immediately I began receiving email messages from all kinds of people in the UGA community expressing their excitement to meet me or work with me. One of the first messages I received came from Rev. Renee DuBose of Our Hope Metropolitan Community Church. I was absolutely thrilled! I literally danced around my living room and squealed, "I'm going to find a church!"

I had heard about Metropolitan Community Churches (MCC) as a denomination that was welcoming to LGBT people. In fact, there reportedly was one just thirty minutes away from where I was living in Michigan. However, based on the experiences I'd had with church and religious people so far, and being the night owl that I am, I just was not invested enough to actually get up extra early on a Sunday to drive thirty minutes to a church that might disappoint me as much as the others had. But now, there would be a congregation right in Athens and I was so excited to check it out.

Another email came from a woman who had attended the open forum that was held during my visit to campus. Katy was the sexual health coordinator in UGA's health services department and was still pretty new to the university, having been there less than six months. Having moved from out of state herself, she offered to help with apartment searching by visiting properties for me to scope them out and send photos if they looked promising. Katy would become one of my closest and dearest friends during my time in Athens.

The following Friday was the staff retreat with the Department of Intercultural Affairs. While I was there I stayed with Corey, one of the faculty members who had been on the search committee that hired me, and his husband, Yancey. They had a beautiful home that friends affectionately called the Barbie Dream House. They generously offered to let me to stay with them for a few weeks if I needed a place to land in order to avoid making a rushed decision and being stuck in a lease for a year. Almost daily I was receiving welcoming messages, emails about housing opportunities, and people sharing their excitement about my arrival. I was overwhelmed by their kindness and was definitely feeling anointed with God's blessings.

I had every intention of finding an apartment while I was there. Katy had even picked me up and taken me to a few properties on Friday after the retreat. Unfortunately, I had no luck finding what I was looking for. I returned to Corey and Yancey's that evening, exhausted, excited, and overwhelmed. The next morning, I woke up to dreary, rainy weather that felt more like late October than early August - especially in Georgia. I had this feeling of overwhelming dread and anxiety. I couldn't help pondering, *what have I done?* and, *have I made a mistake?* I also definitively knew there was no turning back. I was so incredibly scared that morning that it almost didn't seem real.

Corey dropped me off at my supervisor's house who was to transport me back to the Atlanta airport. I felt so overwhelmed with emotions that it was difficult to carry on a conversation. Although I had really enjoyed my interactions with her so far, she did not really know me. While our personalities seemed to have quickly clicked, given that she was my direct supervisor, I wasn't exactly sure at that point just how vulnerable I could be with her. All I could think about was that the only thing left to do at home was to say farewell to the place that had become the only home I'd known for almost twelve years and the people who had loved me into my authentic self when members of my own family couldn't. It made for a long ride to the airport.

As it turned out, the morning that I was to pack up all of my things from my apartment into a moving truck, I woke with the same overwhelming feelings of dread and anxiety. But, this time I was in my own apartment and there wasn't the pressure to hold it together that there had been at the

Barbie Dream House. I laid in my bed that morning, tears streaming down my face before my head ever rose off the pillow. Incidentally, the weather outside was exactly the same as it had been a few days before in Georgia - grey, gloomy, and rainy. I was completely overwhelmed. I was picking up my whole life and moving to a new place that was at least a day's drive away from home, where I knew no one, and had no permanent place to live. Although I'd always been a pretty independent person, even as a child, this new endeavor was beginning to feel insurmountable, even for me. Desperate for some consolation, I picked up my phone and called my ex-girlfriend for some comforting words. She had just made a similar move from Michigan to Savannah and that was really what had inspired me to apply for this particular job in the first place.

She tried to assure me that the emotions I was experiencing were perfectly normal, that she'd been scared too, and that I would be fine once I got there. While I appreciated her effort, it did not ease my mind nor my heart. After hanging up with her I cried some more before forcing myself out of the bed to try and start getting things together. My uncle and his brother would be arriving soon with the moving van and I needed to get my shit together. As I got out of the bed and tried to dry my tears, the overwhelming fear and anxiety combined with the sadness of leaving a place that had become home for me, was more than my heart and mind could handle.

Suddenly overcome with my emotions, for the first time in my life, I found myself on my knees in desperation. I'd gone from frantic to fragile and in that moment I begged for God to soothe my soul. I took a break from trying to figure everything out and allowed myself to just breathe. At that point it felt like that was all I could manage to do. Within moments a sense of peace washed over my entire being. The fear that had been so heavy on my heart was lifted and I was suddenly able to focus on the task at hand. As I picked myself up off the floor, I realized that within minutes God had provided me with exactly what I so desperately needed and had asked for, and I knew that everything was going to be okay.

CHAPTER EIGHTEEN
Everything's Always Working Out

After a daylong affair of packing my things onto the moving van and doing a final cleaning of the apartment, I put both kitties in the car and headed to Detroit to spend the night with my best friend, Jenny. The next morning, we got up, packed the kitties back in the car and Jenny and I began the 18-hour trip to Athens. Along the way, we stopped for the night at my sister's house in Tennessee which was just about four hours from our destination. To be clear, my destination at that point was broadly Athens, as I still had not secured a place to live. The back-up plan was to stay with Corey and Yancey at the Barbie Dream House until I could find a place, but they had two dogs. My fear was that the stress of being cooped up in a car for a day and a half only to be brought into a space that was occupied by dogs would put my cats over the edge. That, and the idea of moving again in a matter of weeks, was more than my spirit could handle.

So, as we left my sister's house that morning for the last leg of our trip, Jenny's job was to find me an apartment. I had picked up some apartment guides on my visit less than a week earlier, and she was methodically going through all of the properties eliminating those that did not allow pets, those that were too high in rent, and those that didn't have a washer and dryer. By the time we arrived early that afternoon, she had come up with three properties that looked promising and that we could view that day. The last location we visited was perfect.

They had two open units, one of which was available for move-in immediately, the other was not available until the following morning as they were finishing up some painting. As a single woman living alone, I had my mind set on the two-story townhouse as I hated the idea of sleeping on the ground floor. Of course, that was the unit that would not be ready until the next day. Exhausted from the chaos of the last few weeks and feeling *so* close to the finish line, and particularly dreading the thought of taking my cats into the Barbie Dream House even for the night, I was tempted to just take the flat that was immediately available for occupancy. As Jenny and I stood in the unit discussing my dilemma about the cats, something happened that blew my mind.

Overhearing our conversation and my concerns about the kitties, the leasing agent said, "If you really want the townhouse, you could leave your cats in the unoccupied flat overnight until we can get you into this unit." Stunned at the helpfulness of this offer, I paused to process what she had just said.

"You mean I could leave the cats in the other unit that I'm not going to rent?" I asked for clarification.

"Yes. You have a litter box or something for them to

use?" She asked.

"Yes, I do."

"Yeah, I don't see why that would be a problem then. You would just need to make sure the unit is clean when you take them out, but that way you don't have to worry about taking them to your friend's house with the dogs."

"Really? Oh my gosh, that would be amazing! You're sure it's not a problem?" I asked, still in disbelief that she was offering a solution to my dilemma that had nothing to do with her or the unit. It was pretty clear that I was going to rent one unit or the other, and it was clear that my cats had another place to go. This woman had no obligation to help me out. Perhaps this was my first taste of true Southern hospitality, but I've also come to believe that this was another small example of God's touch on my journey.

"Not at all! Let me get you the keys to that unit and we can get them settled in right now," the leasing agent said before disappearing off to the office.

She returned with the keys and sent us on our way to the other unit where we unloaded the kitties and tried to make them as comfortable as possible in a completely empty apartment. I promised them we'd be back as early as possible the next day to move them to their real home. Jenny and I then headed to the Barbie Dream House for an evening of dinner and drinks with new friends.

The next morning we rose early and headed over to get the kitties and then to the office to exchange the keys for my two-story townhouse, where the unpacking of the truck commenced. It felt so exciting to be in a brand new, two-bedroom place that was all mine. While moving is always stressful, I think the best part is the feeling of a fresh start. While Jenny and I moved most of the things, that afternoon some of the students who had been part of the search committee who hired me also came over and helped to finish unpacking the truck. This gave me a sense that they were very excited about my arrival and I felt even more excited about my job. I mean, let's be real, who really enjoys helping someone move?

These small blessings early on in my Athens experience where indicators for me of the charmed experiences to come.

CHAPTER NINETEEN
Guided to Greatness

The next morning was my first day on campus. As a newcomer, my parking structure was located on the opposite side of the student union from the building my office was in. It was a beautiful, balmy morning as I made my way toward Tate Plaza. As I got closer to Sanford Drive and began climbing the stairs to the street level, the prestigious Sanford Stadium slowly came into view and it was awe-inspiring in its magnitude. The mammoth stadium was situated directly next to Memorial Hall where my office was located. My heart leapt with excitement as I reached the top of the stairs and took in the surreal sight of the stadium glistening in the sun. I crossed the street and walked onto the bridge that provided a full view into the stadium. "*I'm at the University of Georgia,*" I whispered to myself in amazement.

After having that dramatic moment, I proceeded next door into Memorial Hall. I was greeted with a handmade banner hanging above the LGBT Resource Center door that the students had made to welcome me. I felt like I was in a movie. To feel so anticipated and welcomed by an entire community was something I'd never experienced before. It was perfectly indicative of how my entire time in Athens would be.

One of the interesting things to me about the South is a thing called Southern charm or Southern hospitality which is a culture of being incredibly warm and welcoming to visitors. While in most cases this was typically genuine, it also made for an environment in which I could never be completely sure whether certain people really liked me and the work I was there to do or if they were just being "hospitable." In fact, there were one or two people within my department that made me wonder about their feelings about my office being a part of theirs. However, those people were few and far between and in positions that did not have any influence over my position or office. All of the people who had any kind of supervision, authority, or influence over my work seemed to all be Heaven-sent.

My direct supervisor was incredibly supportive both professionally and personally and our weekly one-on-one meetings quickly became one of my favorite times of the week. The Vice President of Student Affairs, who my supervisor reported to, had a reputation as a champion for the LGBT Resource Center and seemed very invested in the work of the office and protecting it from any kind of political interference. Corey and a number of other faculty members who had done an incredible amount of work on behalf of the LGBTQ community at UGA were all quick to reach out to me and make it known that they were ready and willing to support me in my position and the Center in any way that would be helpful. And then there was Dr. Willie Banks.

While all of these other folks seemed excited to work with me and about what I brought to the position, there was something special about Willie. Although he had officially been a member of the search committee that hired me, somehow I had not had an opportunity to interact with him prior to my first day of work on campus. However, on that first day, he and another colleague from Campus Life came over to my office specifically to welcome me. Although I'd never laid eyes on him before, he immediately made me feel like I was the best thing since sliced bread. His affection for me felt so genuine, and to this day he is one of my favorite people.

Over time, I came to understand that this was Willie's nature - loving people into their potential. In retrospect, I realize this didn't necessarily have anything to do with me specifically, in the same way that my supervisor, the VP, and Corey and other queer faculty members would have rallied behind anyone who had been hired for the position. However, it was not lost on me that I was led to my dream job in a place that seemed to be full of people who were so invested in the work I would be doing. Despite not knowing me at all, they anticipated nothing but greatness from me in this position. In doing so, they held a space for me to graciously step into that greatness. When I doubted myself, their perception of me was there to light the way on my Journey.

In case I missed those cues, there were other, what I like to call, "winks from the Universe" along the way that would always reassure me that I was right where I was supposed to be. Like when the IT person came to set up my computer and my email on my first day of work and the default password she assigned to me was "precious1." And when the second football game of my first fall semester was a non-conference game against Central Michigan University. That had never happened before nor since, but it provided me an opportunity to reconnect and visit with colleagues from CMU who had come to Athens for the game. It felt like family coming to visit me in my new home just weeks after getting settled, which was an incredibly comforting experience after having navigated so much uncertainty in the process of physically moving there. These kinds of Divine communications would happen throughout my entire Athens experience. I gradually became better at not only recognizing them but also interpreting them and trusting them to lead me on my Journey.

CHAPTER TWENTY

Finding My People

Perhaps the biggest blessing of my time in Athens was finding Our Hope Metropolitan Community Church. For years I'd been searching for something larger than myself, something to believe in. I would think, *there's got to be more to life than this.* However, I had yet to find the place to really explore that.

After having received one of my first "welcome to Athens" emails from Rev. Renee DuBose of Our Hope MCC, I was so excited at the thought of finally finding a church home. While the church I had been attending before leaving Michigan had been comfortable, there still was this uncertainty about how they might treat me if they knew I was a lesbian. MCC was a denomination that was founded by a gay man. There was no question about whether I would be fully welcomed. There was this deep sense of knowing that I was about to find my people.

I think it was my second Sunday in Athens when I made my first visit. The church did not have its own building, but rented space from the Presbyterian Student Center. It was a small, intimate space, seating maybe 50-60 people, with an aisle down the middle. The altar was elevated about a foot above the ground and fully accessible. There was a small group of chairs off to the right on the elevated altar that were for the members of the choir. There was a piano and a song leader who led the group.

One of the things that stood out to me immediately about the service was the serving of Communion. I learned that unlike most denominations including the one I had been sporadically raised in, which serve Communion every fifth Sunday, MCC churches celebrate Communion every Sunday. At each service, they explain that there are no barriers or prerequisites to receiving Communion. You don't have to be a member of that church or any church. You don't have to have been baptized or even "saved." All that is required is that you have a willingness to come and receive God's blessing. Not only that, but they served grape juice instead of wine so as not to prevent those who might be in recovery from partaking in this sacred ritual. I found this incredibly inclusive and intentional and I loved everything about it. Yet when the time came in the service that I had the opportunity to receive communion, I did not participate. There were a few reasons why I think I did not immediately partake. The first was that, never having been baptized, I had never received Communion before. It had been explained to me that in the Southern Baptist tradition, baptism was something that each individual had to come to on their own. They did not Christen babies but kids only needed to declare Jesus Christ their Lord and Savior to initiate their baptism.

Although I had not been baptized, I had once experienced what I now recognize as Validation Tears when I was very young and the adults made quite a big deal of it. It was during what they called a "revival meeting," which, as an adult, I've come to learn is "a series of services held to inspire active members of the church body to gain new converts." Thank you, Wikipedia.

I was led to the altar where many members were on their knees praying aloud. The prayers would start as a soft murmur and gradually crescendo until some people were literally shouting their prayers. The man who was preaching knelt down so that he was face to face with me and asked me some questions. He asked if I accepted Jesus as my Lord and Savior. At the time, I didn't really understand what that meant, but I could sense that the correct answer was "yes."

I definitely didn't understand at that moment that I was being "saved." It wasn't until after the roaring of the praying had subsided that the man announced to the room praises to God for the saving of my soul. I still didn't really know what that meant, which, I guess is probably why I was never baptized as a child. What I did understand was that you did not get to receive Communion if you have not been baptized. So, although I heard the MCC clergy loud and clear about there being no conditions to receiving, I think I still felt like I somehow was not worthy of participating.

Another part of me was curious about how it worked. The perfectionist in me who is not comfortable with new things wanted the opportunity to observe the ritual before participating in it. I watched quietly as the ushers released each row to go to the altar where the pastor and a few other servers stood with a plate of wafers and a goblet of grape juice, the symbols of the body and blood of Christ. As each person approached, they were given a wafer which they then dipped into the goblet of grape juice before placing it in their mouth. Having been to a Catholic mass with a friend's family when I was young, where I unwittingly took Communion, was relieved that at MCC everyone wasn't drinking out of the same cup. After eating the wafer dipped in the juice, there was the option for the prayer minister to pray with you, which for me was the weirdest, most uncomfortable aspect. Interestingly this would later become my favorite moment of the service.

My first time ever visiting an MCC church brought me both joy and dissonance to see so many same-sex couples in a place of worship. At some point during the service, Rev Renee made a point to welcome me as the new director of the LGBT Resource Center. This actually happened pretty frequently at almost every event I showed up to, and I quickly began to feel like a local celebrity. I had invited a colleague that I had befriended who had started working at the university just weeks before I had to join me that day. Given that it was a "gay church" many people assumed she and were together, which was awkward. I think the fact that I'm super femme and she was more on the masculine end of the spectrum in terms of our appearance contributed to people's assumptions as I looked around the room and observed several binary, lesbian couples. By "binary" I mean that one of the pair seemingly presents more masculine while the other presents more feminine, mirroring the societal norm of heterosexuality. Some people also refer to this as heteronormative.

Following the service, we were invited to join a group of members of the church for lunch at a local establishment. I respectfully declined that day. I was still feeling a bit like a fish out of water. While I had enjoyed the service and certainly intended to return for another, I was also not ready to jump head first into the deep end. After all, most of my adult life, I had believed that a relationship with God was elusive for someone like me. So, to suddenly consider the extreme opposite as a possibility, and be surrounded by people who fully believed in the viability of God's unconditional love, despite their sexuality…well, that was just a lot to process all at once.

I had spent so much of my life dismissing people who believed in God and talked about their faith as people who were anti-gay. The thought of now associating with self-proclaimed gay Christians, and especially the potential that they might want me to become one, was just a little more than I was ready for. In fact, at that point, I think there was probably still a part of me that had internalized the spiritual violence and homophobia that I had experienced during my coming out, and I wasn't sure that I necessarily believed that this "gay church" could be a legit thing. Although I declined the lunch invitation, I assured them I would be back for next week's service.

CHAPTER TWENTY-ONE
Learning to Pray

As promised, I returned to Our Hope the following Sunday. Although I did not immediately create a habit of attending, I did attend about once or twice a month during my first year in Athens. It was refreshing to always be welcomed just as enthusiastically as I had been on my initial visit.

There were a core group of church members that were almost always in attendance. These folks would eventually become some of my dearest friends that I would lovingly refer to as my church family. Tommie, in particular, was like a one-woman welcoming committee. She and her wife, Patty, had been married nearly fifteen years and Tommie was the type that never met a stranger. She took joy in providing a loving, maternal energy to younger people who did not necessarily have the support of their own parents. She was a bit of a self-proclaimed Momma Bear but was also not afraid to provide some tough love in any given situation. Through the years, I really appreciated her candor and direct communication.

By my second or third visit, I was ready to receive Communion. All it took was one time to completely change my initial impression. On my first visit to Our Hope, I had felt a little uncomfortable as I watched people pray together. The prayer ministers would lovingly wrap the person they were praying with in a hug. Having never seen this done in any other church, it struck me as oddly intimate. Still, I had a desire to fully participate in this experience of church. Despite some hesitation, I trusted the proclamation that there were no prerequisites and approached the altar to receive Communion. I came to realize there was something incredibly moving about partnering with another human - many times an acquaintance, at best - and for them to pray for me. That was definitely something I'd never experienced before and moved me to tears. It was also how I learned to pray.

I realize now that this may sound silly to some people, but there was a time when I thought I didn't know how to pray. I felt like there was some formal, ceremonious, or "appropriate" way to approach God that eluded me. More importantly, I didn't know what to say. I think I thought that if I'm talking to God, I need to be asking him for very big, important, life-altering things. Like, mundane, day to day things, were not worth God's time or attention. I think that this is what made weekly Communion so special to me. After receiving the elements of Communion, I never passed up the opportunity to have a prayer minister pray with me. Through these experiences, those people taught me to pray.

My favorite prayer minister was Tony. Tony was a

beautiful, spiritual, Black man with a spirit that beamed from his being. He had a gorgeous smile and a singing voice that I'd swear was an oracle for the Holy Spirit. It was a rare occasion that Tony could get through an entire song without having brought me to tears. His faith and belief and connection to the Divine was palpable as he prayed with me in his arms. And when he prayed with me, it was always as if he was Divinely downloading exactly what I needed to hear.

Communion, especially with Tony, was also one of the first places where I recognized God's communication with me. Although Tony was exceptionally gifted when it came to asking God for exactly what I needed, more often than not, whatever prayer minister I ended up with would somehow always know just what to pray for with me. As someone who felt like she didn't know how to pray or what to pray for, it was always magical when someone who did not know the intricate details of my life would connect with me and the things that they asked God to provide me spoke exactly to what I was needing in my life. Sometimes, I didn't even know I needed the thing they were praying for until I heard them pray it over me and here came the Validation Tears. Eventually, it occurred to me that they knew exactly what to pray for because God already knew exactly what I needed. It was through their words that God was letting *me* know He was with me. So, interestingly, although they were talking to God on my behalf, it seemed to me that God was talking to me through their words.

Similarly, I would experience these Validation Tears during some of the messages preached during the service. Particularly when I was dealing with something in my personal life, there would be times when it seemed as if the message being preached had been prepared specifically for me. In those cases, the message was always something that I desperately needed to hear, that gave me guidance, and that showed me something about myself and/or my situation. Our Hope MCC was a loving, close-knit community. Almost without fail, anytime I experienced these tears, at least one person would approach me after the service to make sure everything was alright and try to comfort me. For a long time it was hard to explain to people, because I didn't yet understand it myself. I would simply tell them I was fine and thank them for their concern.

Gradually, and during more challenging times of my life, those tears became more and more common, and I learned that people are generally super uncomfortable with tears. Friends who meant well would insist I come sit near them and try to soothe my tears through the service. Eventually, this really frustrated me. I think that is how I began to recognize that this emotion I was experiencing was a gift from God - the Divine letting me know that I am never alone and that when I pay attention, I will come to understand. The tears are God's way of getting my attention and making sure I get the message, and making me aware that I also know what I need when I am still and listen.

CHAPTER TWENTY-TWO
Inspiration Incarnate

I had been in Athens for about a year when Our Hope MCC celebrated their 10-year anniversary. As part of the celebration, Rev. Dr. Troy Perry, the founder of the Metropolitan Community Church denomination, visited the church for the weekend. They held a couple different events in which he was the guest of honor. In addition to finding some comfort and connection at Our Hope, I also experienced a bit of internal conflict about the idea of it being a "gay church." Some part of me had internalized my dad's homophobia and the spiritual violence I had experienced which caused me, on some level, to question the legitimacy of a "gay church" like the Metropolitan Community Church.

I had also become aware of a sense of some level of expectation, related to my professional position, to participate and support the church. Prior to Rev. Perry's arrival that weekend, Rev. Renee had reached out to me weeks before to help spread the word about the events. Not knowing anything about Rev. Troy Perry, I obliged and helped to market the various events to our students. While most of the events were open to the campus and local community, there was one gathering that was specifically for members of the church. It was an evening gathering over a meal with Rev. Perry.

During his time with us, Rev. Perry told us the story of the founding of the denomination. I was mesmerized as I listened. Having been raised in the Pentecostal church, he shared with us that he had a heart for God from the time he was a little boy and was passionately involved in the church. He had begun preaching at an exceptionally young age as a teenager and eventually became a clergy member. However, after coming out as gay, he was defrocked. Having been seen as a leader in the church and told by others his whole life that God had a ministry for him, this was understandably devastating. At some point, he moved to California and experienced a break-up that left him in a terrible depression. Feeling completely lost and disconnected from God, he attempted to take his own life. It was through that experience that he reconnected with God and began to wake up to his Calling to create a church with an outreach to gay and lesbian people.

He began talking with friends about his vision and was met mostly with skepticism. There were a few friends however, who had connections that helped him follow his "crazy dream." It was the fall of 1968 when he was able to convince the editors of The Advocate to sell him an ad promoting his first church service which would be held in his living room. He didn't know what to expect, but 12 people met that day for that first service. It was a small but diverse group, and it was an emotional experience for everyone who attended. The church continued to meet each Sunday, growing by a few people each week. Eventually, they had to move the service from location to location in order to keep accommodating the growth of the group.

He shared with us, in detail, the trials and tribulations that he and the growing church experienced and overcame over the years, including one church that was burned to the ground by people who opposed MCC's message. It was a fascinating and inspirational story. I felt so incredibly blessed to be in the presence of a person who had not only followed his Calling in the face of such adversity, but who had blessed me and so many others across the world with the gift of God's unconditional love through his work and I took the opportunity to tell him so. It was an incredibly emotional experience for me and one I will always remember. Rev. Perry continues to inspire me as I navigate following my own Calling of sharing my Spiritual Journey with others regardless and in spite of the naysayers I will certainly encounter along the way.

Following this monumental experience, I became more actively involved in the church and participating in the weekly service. Some weeks I was an usher, greeting new and familiar faces at the door, lighting the ceremonial candles on the altar at the start of service and ushering out the Light of the Holy Spirit at the end of service. Other weeks I served as an acolyte assisting with serving Communion. My favorite role, though, was reading the Scriptures at the start of service. Maybe it was the public speaker in me, or maybe it was just my thing for words, but I enjoyed "calling the service to order" with the reading of the Gospel.

I found that in this space, as I had found with pretty much all of Athens, I was openly embraced by people. It was evident that people in the church and the community found the work that I was blessed with leading at the university incredibly important and I felt nothing but love and support from every direction. In that regard, my role at The University of Georgia and my experiences there felt incredibly Divine and my life felt completely in "flow." During an interview with the campus paper about my position, I once explained this feeling as "I am what I do and I do what I am." To me, it is no coincidence that I found this spiritual community at Our Hope MCC when I did.

CHAPTER TWENTY-THREE
The Only Validation I Need

While my professional life and even my personal life in Athens felt very charmed and like I was precisely where I was supposed to be, there was continued conflict with my extended family over my sexual orientation. I had always been very close to my aunt Stacie growing up. I was the oldest grandchild on my dad's side of the family. Only nine years old when I was born, Stacie had always been more like a sister to me than an aunt. Since both my parents were very young when I was born and working full-time to make ends meet, she babysat me a lot. I have fond memories of playing restaurant with her in which she would "take my order" and deliver my lunch. Incidentally, lunch was always a grilled cheese sandwich. She was my best friend and my favorite person. I was a flower girl in her wedding. A couple years later I cried the entire hour-ride home, heartbroken after she and my uncle Mitch delivered the news that they would be moving to Tennessee.

Over the next several years, through junior high and high school, I kept in touch with Stacie and Mitch through written letters, and we would make a family trip down to visit them at least once or twice a year. My sister and I both loved those trips. For the first few years, they would also make trips up to visit us. Regardless of whether it was here or there, we always loved our time with them. However, after returning from Disney and my dad reacting so negatively about my relationship with Tawnny, I knew that I could not - nor did I want to - discuss it with Stacie. So, rather than lie or tell half-truths about what was going on in my life, I limited my contact with her. That was fairly easy to do given that they lived in Tennessee and I lived in Michigan. Also, at the same time that I was "busy with college" they were having kids and getting acclimated to having a family of their own. To this day, Stacie and I have never had a verbal conversation about my sexuality.

A few years after my dad passed away, my sister graduated from high school and moved to Tennessee where she lived for a few years before marrying and starting a family of her own. About a month after the anniversary celebration at Our Hope MCC, I was making a trip to Tennessee to surprise my sister for a visit. I had let my aunt Stacie know that I was coming so that she could help to coordinate the surprise. Stacie sent a text inviting me to stay at their house if I needed a place to stay. I replied thanking her for the offer but letting her know that I was bringing a friend with me and had already booked a hotel room. Although I got an initial reply saying okay, the next day I got another text stating that she and my uncle Mitch loved me very much and would love to visit with me but that "we are concerned about you bringing your friend...the kids are old enough now to figure some things out and I think it would put all of us in an awkward position."

I experienced a series of emotions. I immediately felt shocked. I had never intended to have a conversation with them about my sexuality - that's why I'd spent so many years avoiding them! Then, I felt incredibly hurt. It was like I was going through the same emotions I had felt with my dad all over again. I'd always felt so loved and adored by them and now, this one thing about me had somehow overshadowed all their other feelings and created this situation of conditional love. Then, I got pissed. My text to her had simply said I was bringing "a friend." I had not specified if that friend was a man or a woman. Additionally, I used the word "friend" and she had jumped to the conclusion that this friend was someone I was dating. To be fair, Angela was more than a friend - but that was not the point. Stacie wouldn't even say directly what it was she thought the kids would be so savvy to "figure out." She was speaking in some kind of code about something she'd never thought important enough to approach me about before, but now wanted to make an issue of without even having all the information. And what did she think we were going to do, make out on her couch??

This text exchange led to an email correspondence in which she shared with me that she had never changed her beliefs from the time she was a little girl and the day she got saved at age seven. She also mentioned how she knew that I wasn't brought up in church, and so maybe it was hard for me to understand, that as an older figure in my life, she would hope I had enough confidence in her to do what was right. She went on to say that she knew my dad would expect nothing less of her. This last statement was perhaps the most hurtful part.

I was devastated. I closed the door to my office and called my cousin Jason, who is the second grandchild, the oldest grandson, and also gay. When he was younger, prior to coming out to his mom, he had also moved to Tennessee for a stint and lived with Stacie and Mitch.

"Have you ever had a conversation with Stacie about the fact that you're gay?" I asked him.

"No, I was kinda hoping I would never have to," Jason replied. He has a much drier sense of humor than I and far more tolerance for the homophobic bullshit my aunt was dishing. I relayed to him the text and email exchange, and I sobbed as I realized that this "conversation" was finally happening and I was feeling hopeless about coming to any kind of understanding with her.

"Jennifer, you know that's just how they are. It doesn't mean they don't love you or want to see you. I know that they love you very much. They just don't love *that* about you. But you're never going to change their minds about it," Jason told me. In that moment it felt like he was defending Stacie and Mitch, but I now realize he was just much better at allowing than I was at that point in time.

"Well that's not going to work for me. They cannot pick and choose the parts of me that they love. They either love all of me or they don't. I cannot compartmentalize the various aspects of who I am, nor should I have to. If they can't love all of me, then they can't love any of me," I indignantly declared.

Ultimately, Angela - who, ironically, I had met at church - and I went to Tennessee that weekend and visited my sister and her family, but we did not visit Stacie and Mitch. My sister was well aware of my identity and had been for years. She had met all of my girlfriends except Tawnny and had always been very supportive. Like Jason, my exchange with Stacie had not surprised her. For me, it seemed to bring all the emotions I'd gone through with my dad back to the surface. While there was a time that I had felt somewhat vindicated by my dad's declaration of "If I'm wrong, God strike me dead!" followed by his subsequent death, Stacie's declaration about my dad's expectations to reject my sexual orientation really caused me to question the legitimacy of MCC. There were times when I wondered if I was naive to believe that what they were preaching was true. That God's love really was for everyone.

While I was there that weekend, I struggled about whether or not I could visit with my grandmother, who lived just across the border into Kentucky. She and I had been having fairly regular phone conversations over the previous few months. I had been looking forward to visiting with her in-person since I hadn't had a lot of time with her as an adult. Because my trip was a surprise, I had not let her know I was coming to town. Now, given the nature of my email exchange with Stacie, I was worried that they may have talked and that she, too, might be upset. I had asked Stacie in our email exchange if she and Grandma had ever talked about the fact that I might be gay, but Stacie had not responded to that question. I sat on the bed in the hotel room, turning my cell phone over in my hand, trying to decide if I should reach out to her or not. Angela encouraged me to just do it.

"Just call her! She's your grandma. You can't come all this way and not visit with her," she said. "I will stay here and hang out at the hotel if that would be easier for you. I don't want you to miss out on time with her."

"No. That's dumb. I did not invite you to come with me so that you could hang out in a hotel room by yourself," I replied.

Just as I was saying this, my phone rang in my hand. It was my grandma. My heart stopped for a second.

"It's my grandma!" I said, frozen with anxiety about whether to answer it.

"Answer it!" she insisted.

I let it ring three and half times before I finally picked it up.

"Hello?" I answered, my heart still racing.

"Jennifer?" my Grandma replied.

"Hi, Grandma."

"How are you?" she asked.

"I'm fine, how are you?" I replied, happy to hear her voice and trying to not be nervous about the conversation.

"I'm good...I know you're in Tennessee," she said playfully, letting me know she wanted to see me.

"You do?" I said, feigning surprise.

"Yes, I do!" She said in a you-can't-get-nothin-by-me manner.

"You know I wouldn't come all this way and not visit you." I said.

"Well, I hope not!" my Grandma replied.

Clearly, Stacie had talked to her, that's how she knew I was in town. What I didn't know was whether Stacie had filled her in on our exchange about my "friend."

"You know, I was just about to call you when my phone rang. I have a .friend with me and I wanted to make sure it was ok that I bring her when I stop by." I closed my eyes and held my breath as I waited for her reply.

"Well, yeah, that's okay," she replied. I still couldn't read her tone enough to get a sense of whether she knew about my conversation with Stacie.

"Ok, well, I just wanted to check. I know how y'all are about unannounced company!" I teased. She laughed and I told her we would be leaving shortly to head over to see her.

It was about a forty-five minute drive across the mountain to my Grandma's house. I was more and more nervous the closer we got. All the way there I was contemplating whether or not Stacie would have mentioned what was going on to my Grandma or if she had just mentioned to her that I was coming to town. There was a very small part of me that even worried about it being an ambush of sorts. Like she knew what was going on and wanted to see me to share with me her disapproval. But then I would remember the conversation we had just before we got in the car to head over there and it definitely didn't feel like that was something she would do. I was nervous because I really had no idea what to expect when we arrived.

My grandma lived in a cozy house on the side of a mountain in the hills of Kentucky. There was a steep, windy driveway that was flanked by the side of the mountain on one side and a deep ravine on the other. At the top of the driveway in front of the house, there was room to turn your vehicle around because backing down it would be a bad idea. As we got out of the car and headed to the wrap-around covered porch, my Grandma met us at the door. She greeted me with a hug and invited us in to sit down.

I sat on the couch and Angela sat on the sofa across the room. Grandma offered us coffee as was customary to do when you have guests in the South. Then we all sat in the living room and visited for a while. My grandma seemed very comfortable and was very friendly to Angela. At some point there came a lull in the conversation and Angela asked my grandma, "So, how did you know Jennifer was in Tennessee?" My heart stopped and my eyes got big as I shot Angela a look that said, "*WHAT are you doing?*"

I think my grandma had a similar reaction. She had been coming back from the kitchen after refilling her own coffee when Angela asked the question. I could see a hesitation in her body that was almost a full stop, and she looked at Angela in a way that immediately made me feel like Stacie had definitely outed me to her. She paused almost as if she was trying to decide how she wanted this conversation to go and then replied.

"Well, Stacie told me," she said in a matter-of-fact, how-else-would-I-have-known tone, as she continued back to her seat next to me on the couch. I sat holding my breath, praying Angela didn't have any other surprise questions up her sleeve. My grandma sat down and filled the silence.

"Yeah, Stacie told me," she said again and took a sip of her coffee. She then proceeded to talk about how much she loved spending time with me. "It is so good to see you. You know, I don't get to see any of my grandkids and I miss them so much. I just love you'ns so much and I would give anything in this world to get to spend more time with you'ns. All my grandkids."

She went on to talk about how she didn't understand why people hold grudges and that life is too short to let things keep us apart. "We're all gonna have to answer to God for ourselves one day and I just wish I could spend more time with my family."

Her words were kind of rambling in a way that could

have probably been interpreted by different people differently. However, it was clear to me that she was talking about "it" without talking about it. What I came away with was that although she may not have necessarily approved of my relationship, she also recognized that approval was not hers to give. And that, in the grand scheme of things, all of it was between me and God. She just really wanted to spend time with her grandchildren and other family members that may have had some other kinds of disagreements with her.

We visited with my grandma that day for three or four hours. Outside of the heart-stopping question from Angela, it was completely comfortable and pleasant. I left feeling so grateful for that time spent with her. I think it was the only time that I had ever spent with her in person, as an adult, that wasn't a family gathering of some sort.

It was such an eye-opening experience for me. Based on my dad's extreme negative reaction to my relationships with women and now my aunt Stacie's negative reaction, both of which were predicated on their religious beliefs, it seemed only logical to me that my grandmother - their mother would have a similar reaction. After all, she was a much more religious person than my dad had been and attended church every Sunday. The church was her social community and she talked about God all the time. But at the end of the day, my grandma's love for me was more important to her than any judgment or condemnation. She seemed to understand that she was not responsible for my relationship with God

Although I didn't necessarily see it so clearly at the time, that was one of the most powerful gifts she ever gave me.

For years, I was so hurt about the loss of my relationship with Stacie and Mitch. I would contemplate trying to have a conversation with them, trying to win their approval by sharing my experience of God with them. I could imagine all of their objections in my mind: *Of course they're going to tell you being gay is okay - your church was founded by a gay man. Them telling you so doesn't make it true.* I felt completely unequipped to try to have this conversation with them. Even now, I fear that if nothing else, the amount of time that has passed without discussing the issue has calcified their resolve to cling to their convictions. While there are times when I still long for a connection with them, ultimately, I came to realize that the validation I once so desperately thought I needed from them, I found in God.

CHAPTER TWENTY-FOUR
Third Time's a Charm

It was 2010 during my third academic year in Athens when my future husband came strolling back into my life. I received a message from him through Facebook asking for any advice or information I could provide that would be helpful to him as he began to navigate his transition from female to male at his job. Although we'd maintained a loose online friendship over the years, we had not seen each other in person in about six years. However, since she was one of my favorite residents the year I was an RA, I had noticed when Ainsley Best changed her Facebook profile to Ethan Best. I also was not surprised. The last time we had seen each other in person, he already looked much more like an "Ethan" than an "Ainsley."

Ethan had just moved back to Michigan from Florida and had come out to family and friends as male and was ready to come out at work. Knowing the work that I was doing from our connection on social media, he reached out to me as a resource. Although I wasn't able to directly help him with the logistics of navigating his transition at work, I was able to provide him with some resources and point him in the direction of organizations that I thought could be helpful.

Ethan was very open about his transition. He created a YouTube channel where he shared a weekly video documenting his experience which I watched with intrigue. I'd been working closely with students who were transitioning and supporting them through this process. However, witnessing a close friend's personal experience brought a whole new layer of love and respect for the trans community and affirmation of the work I'd been Called to do.

In early 2011, Ethan posted on Facebook that he was looking for recommendations of surgeons to see for his top surgery. I reached out to him with the name of a doctor in Atlanta that I'd learned about from a guy in the local trans community. After doing some initial research, he contacted me and let me know that he'd decided to see that doctor for a consultation. Assuming he didn't have other contacts in Georgia, I offered for him to stay with me in Athens when he came for his appointment. He accepted my invitation and immediately began planning his trip to Georgia.

The weekend that he chose to visit was a busy one. It was the last weekend of April, which the queer community in Athens lovingly refers to as "Gaypril" because of all of the queer events that happen that month. I let him know when he was choosing his travel dates that he was welcome to come but that there would be several events that I would need to be at that weekend, including Athens Pride. I explained that he was welcome to attend all the events with me or not. I just wanted him to know that I would have obligations that weekend. Remembering how things had gone between us historically, I sensed the need to clearly establish boundaries before he got there and made a point to tell him that I did not have a guest bed. We were corresponding via Facebook messenger:

"YAY!!! I'm super excited to see you, too!!! Whiiiich reminds me...I have to clean my apartment! lol Also, not that it matters to me - and hopefully it won't matter to you, but I can't remember if I told you that I don't have a guest bed...I have a super comfy couch which I don't mind sleeping on...and I have my queen size bed which I don't mind sharing - if you can behave yourself! lol 😄 In any case, we'll work it out, but thought I should probably give you a heads up."

"I will take your couch. I can't promise to behave...only because how...well...uh...testosterone...I will sleep on the couch to be safe."

He arrived in Athens that Friday evening by airport shuttle and joined me at a friend's birthday party at a local hotel restaurant. I went out to the parking lot to meet him and put his luggage in my vehicle and remember having a visceral reaction and immediately thinking *Damn. He looks so good!*, and proceeding to do my best to play it cool. That energy that I had noticed emanating from him the last time we'd seen each other in person seemed to somehow be off the charts this time. I couldn't look away as he confidently, yet casually, walked toward me and greeted me with a hug. Unlike the other times we'd met, this felt like a very even, calm, balanced energy.

We proceeded to the party and I introduced him to my friends. I had intentionally chosen a seat that was clearly big enough to seat two so that I wouldn't have to worry about saving him a seat or finding one for him when he arrived. I clearly did not anticipate what it would feel like to share this "loveseat" with him and his energy. While it did, in fact, seat two, it certainly was not made for strangers.

Following the party, we took a walk downtown to find him something to eat since he had arrived after all the tables had been cleared and the party was winding down. It was a beautiful late April evening in Georgia, so the weather was no longer chilly, but definitely not too hot. It was also a Friday night at the end of the semester in a college town, so the streets were abuzz with people enjoying a night on the town. After settling for a burger at Five Guys, we headed back to my place. The next morning was one of the biggest days of the year for me and I wanted to be rested and have everything ready to go.

Throughout the weekend, Ethan elected to attend all of the events going on in my life. On Saturday, he came along to our Lavender Graduation ceremony which was arguably one of the LGBT Resource Center's biggest programs of the year. After spending most of the day at that event, we went back to my apartment and took a nap before heading back downtown for the bicycle road race that was happening. On Sunday morning we headed to church, which was his first experience with Metropolitan Community Church. I enjoyed introducing him to the loving support system that I'd cultivated over the years that I'd been there. After church, we went to the Athens Pride picnic which was another opportunity to introduce him to a whole other group of people as well as reacquaint him with some of the friends he'd already met during his visit.

That evening, I wanted to take him to my favorite place to eat, The Last Resort Grill. Due to the events that had been going on downtown during the weekend, we found that the restaurant didn't open for another hour. In the meantime, we went to my favorite watering hole and had a couple of drinks.

Over the course of the weekend, Ethan had made a few different references to the two other times that I had not so graciously rejected his advances. This is when I discovered that the things that had happened in our past had clearly left more of an emotional bruise than I had ever realized. While he always brought them up in a teasing manner, it was clear to me that there was some truth at the heart of his remarks. I had also found myself noticing a connection with him that was familiar all the way back to our CMU days. Not having dated a male-identified person in well over ten years, I found myself pondering what this was I was feeling.

After being seated at the restaurant and ordering a glass of wine, I felt compelled to apologize for the way I had behaved in the past and any pain I may have caused.

"I'm really sorry about what happened between us so many years ago," I said, almost without thinking. Clearly the wine was preventing me from over analyzing my word choice.

Ethan sat speechless, eyes on me as I continued.

"I never meant to hurt your feelings. As embarrassed as I am to say this, I honestly had forgotten many of the details of those situations until you reminded me. I had no idea how much of an impact they had and I'm really, really sorry. I never meant to hurt your feelings."

Taken aback by my vulnerability and willingness to acknowledge the things that he'd been carrying around for fourteen years, knowingly or not, Ethan paused as he took in my apology.

"Thank you," he said, never breaking eye contact with me. Maintaining direct eye contact was a characteristic of his confidence and intensity that hadn't changed over the fourteen years we'd known each other. "You know, I don't think that I even realized that I'd been holding on to those things until I got here. I mean, it's not like I've been pining over you all these years or anything. But coming here to visit with you, definitely brought those memories back to the front of my mind. So, I definitely came this time with no expectations for anything other than a doctor's consultation!"

I chuckled at his candor about having zero expectations.

"But, despite having no expectations, you have allowed me to really see you this weekend," he went on.

"What do you mean?" I asked.

"You have been so open and real and made me feel so welcome. I've had the opportunity to meet the people in your life, to see where you live and work, and especially to see you do your work and that has been amazing. To see you interact with your students and how important they are to you and the way that they look to you for support. It makes me feel more connected to you than I could ever have imagined. Thank you," he explained.

"You're welcome," I said as I smiled at him. The moment felt intense, so I took a break and had a drink of my wine. It felt good for someone who had known me as more than just the director of the LGBT Resource Center to see my passion in action. I genuinely felt seen.

Our food arrived and the conversation became more casual. We'd had a few glasses of wine in addition to the drinks we'd had at the bar before heading over. It is safe to say we were both feeling a little tipsy. It was at this point that Ethan started hinting at some no strings attached action.

"What is it they say? What happens in Athens, stays in Athens?" He said in a tone that let me know he was only half-joking.

"Umm...you were still upset about what didn't happen fourteen years ago, I'm not sure there's any such thing as casual sex between us," I laughed.

He laughed too, but was undeterred.

"I just want to taste you," he said, looking me directly in the eye with a completely straight face. There was that intensity from 1997 all over again. I felt myself blush.

"You don't even have to do anything. Just let me taste you."

I squinted at him suspiciously from across the table. I wasn't so sure about his ability to keep things casual given our history. I also wasn't so sure about my willingness to not reciprocate. *What if I want to do something?* I wondered to myself as I continued to give him side-eye.

My thoughts were interrupted by the server bringing our bill, but I would have the answer to all of my questions before the night was over.

CHAPTER TWENTY-FIVE
Blissful Surrender

As soon as we left the restaurant I realized that I'd had too much to drink to drive home. We decided to walk to my apartment and take a nap and come back for my car later. It was a beautiful night and I lived less than a mile from where we had dinner. Still, Athens has quite the rolling landscape and so it made for a fun, slightly intoxicated walk home.

Feeling the effects of the drinks we'd had and the uphill walk we'd conquered during the last quarter mile, I plopped down on the couch while Ethan headed to the bathroom. A few minutes later, he came back out and sat right next to me on the couch. I turned and looked at him and returned a sly grin as he leaned in, and gently kissed my right shoulder. When I did not object, he kissed it again, moving a little higher with each kiss as I gently moved my head to allow for more kisses on my neck. He slowly worked his way up and around with those sweet gentle kisses until he made it to my lips. Then, when he gently kissed my lips, it felt as if my heart dropped out of my body. My whole body felt weightless and tingly and each kiss got better and better. Equally impacted by the magic of that first kiss, we came to agree that it was well worth the fourteen-year wait and Ethan spent the second half of his trip sharing my queen size bed with me instead of sleeping on the couch.

The following weekend I was finally graduating with my master's degree from Central Michigan University and so I had made plans to spend time with him while I was in Michigan. He came to see me receive my degree on Saturday and I invited him to join me at Metropolitan Community Church of Detroit (MCCD) for service the next day.

If I had to pinpoint the defining moment in our relationship where we turned a corner and never looked back, that church service would be it. I cannot tell you what the message was or what Scripture they were preaching on. I can't even tell you who was preaching that day. What I do know is that both Ethan and I felt a kind of emotional energy that neither of us could put into words. It was like my Validation Tears in overdrive! We were both moved to tears as we held hands throughout the entire service. It was clear that there was a Divine energy that we shared that day.

Following the service, we sat together in my rental car, me in the driver seat, him in the passenger seat, and tried to process what had just happened. We tried to explain to each other what each of us had felt, but words were hard to come by. What I had realized over the past week, between his visit to Athens and my trip to Michigan was that, although we were much more intimate than we ever had been in the past for whatever reason, I was still holding Ethan at arm's distance. I was still guarded. But after this service, I had thi clear moment of surrender in which I made a conscious decision to lean into that love.

"You know, I've been thinking a lot about us and I realize that I'm still doing this to you," I said, putting my right arm out toward him with my hand up in a stop position. "And, I don't know why. I mean, I know why I did it fourteen years ago...and I kinda know why I did it seven years ago, but...I don't know why I'm still doing it. I enjoy you so much, I love our conversations, I'm super attracted to you, I think you're amazing, I find myself wanting to be with you…" I went on as my eyes caught his. "So, I've decided, I'm just going to let you love me."

This calm smile came over his face. He took in my words and then simply said, "Wow. Thank you."

That night we were out with some friends at a karaoke bar and he and I were dancing when I had the conscious thought, *I'm going to embrace every single thing about him.* I realize that sounds kind of weird. If I'm honest, I'm not sure I completely understood it myself at the time. I know now that my Higher Self was guiding me in that moment. Because Ethan has always seen the world in a completely different way than I have ever seen the world, I was intimidated by his energy. In that moment, I was aware that I still was not completely comfortable with his confidence, his level of vulnerability, direct communication, and even his childlike energy. That exuberance was something that had never felt comfortable to me, even when I was a child, myself. This was part of why I had been continuing to keep him at arm's length. However, my all-knowing Higher Self understood that all of the things about him that made me uncomfortable were precisely the things I was needing in my life in order for me to become Who I came into this life to be.

His spiritual sensitivity is one of the specific characteristics that I embraced in faith and that has made the most significant impact on my life. For most of my adult life and even after I had begun to recognize my Divine experiences with God, I still had a strong, what I like to call, "skeptic brain." It's a common concept and we all have it. Some people refer to it as monkey mind or lizard brain and it is the thing that keeps us from achieving our goals, dreams and purpose. For me, my skeptic brain would prevent me from connecting with Spirit by questioning whether those connections were real or even flat out denying them. I think part of that doubt has been based in my need to be right and to know everything - because if I know everything, there is no need for faith. That doubt was perpetuated by my immediate environment of academia where ideas and theories depended upon evidence to support them. Heaven forbid I believe in something that I couldn't empirically prove was real. I might look like a fool. But Ethan's example of living in faith and in the space of miracles, helps me to see the world so differently. It has become easier to quiet my skeptic brain and suspend my disbelief and begin to see and feel and experience the magic of Spirit.

Over the next two years, Ethan and I would make several trips back and forth between Michigan and Georgia, visiting each other every four to six weeks or so. In the meantime, we established a daily routine of spending time together via phone calls and Skype visits. We talked about anything and everything you can imagine, enjoying the process of getting to know one another intimately while still leading very separate and independent lives. The more time we spent together, the more I came to appreciate his direct communication style, his self-awareness of what he wanted in life, and his very different perspective of the world.

During one of his visits to Georgia, we had taken a walk downtown. Somewhere along the way, as we were walking underneath a low-hanging branch that was still just out of my reach, I playfully ran, jumped, and swatted with all my might at the nearest leaf I could reach. This was not a typical practice for me, so I have no idea what compelled me to do it, but Ethan's reaction was totally unexpected and taught me a lot about him.

"Whoa! Why'd you do that?!" Ethan exclaimed.

Like a child that knew they'd done something wrong, but didn't understand exactly what, I said, "Do what?"

"Why did you hit that tree like that?" He asked.

"I don't know...I was just being playful," I replied.

"How would you like it if that tree reached out and smacked you like that?" He asked.

I laughed uncertainly, not knowing for sure if he was

genuinely outraged or if he was being dramatic just to give me a hard time. We had had previous conversations about his belief that inanimate objects had emotions. I shared a similar notion, however, he had been the first and only person I'd ever discussed it with. So, while I had explored the idea in my mind, I had clearly not given it the kind of thought and legitimacy that Ethan had. I found myself suddenly feeling bad and embarrassed for being so insensitive to the tree. This was one of the most revealing interactions we'd had. This moment allowed me to see how differently he viewed the world. Suddenly he gave me a perspective to consider.

During another visit when I traveled to Michigan to visit him, he surprised me with a visit to a healing center where his sister worked. We both received massages, craniosacral therapy, and energy healing. While I had experienced a massage before, craniosacral therapy and energy healing were both new experiences for me. During my energy healing session, the practitioner shared with me her intuitive insight about what was going on for me energetically. During both of these treatments, I experienced the inexplicable emotion that I hadn't yet identified as Validation Tears.

Over and over, we would have experiences like these and conversations that always opened up my mind and heart to a whole new way of seeing things. Actually, if I'm honest, they weren't all new to me. I had simply been too skeptical to embrace or believe in many of them. My initial reaction to something that was so different from my way of thinking was often dismissive or even critical. However, because I had committed to embracing everything about Ethan, I allowed myself to explore things that I otherwise might not have. I loved and respected Ethan so much that I would find myself accepting the idea or concept as *his* perspective and therefore being more open to considering how I felt about that concept. Sometimes my respect for the concept was purely out of my respect for him. But eventually, I found myself contemplating my own views and gradually, becoming more and more open to what we affectionately refer to as "hummina hummina." These were things that are so calming and comforting and magical that they are indescribable. Many seeds were planted on my spiritual journey over these two years that we lived apart, but the real blossoming and spiritual transformation would happen when I finally made the decision to return to Michigan for good.

CHAPTER TWENTY-SIX
There's No Place Like Home...
Don't Make Me Go

When I left Michigan for my dream job in Georgia in 2008, I thought I would never come back. I felt like I had turned a corner and had evolved into that successful person who was going to go out and change the world. At that point, I couldn't imagine ever leaving my new position, much less to go back to Michigan. However, living more than 700 miles away from the one you love can have a very powerful effect on one's life decisions.

Ethan and I had gotten engaged in October of 2011, just six months after his first visit to Athens. We knew at some point, we would end up in the same place, but had not initially been in a rush to figure that out. However, although we were fortunate enough to have the resources to be able visit each other about every 4-6 weeks, the geographical distance eventually started to get old. We discussed the option for him to move to Georgia, however, due to his work situation, it really wasn't ideal. I was working and living in Athens, which - on a good traffic day - was still a hour and a half from where he would have been working in Atlanta. There were multiple conditions that would have to align to even orchestrate a transfer for him and in the event that he did get the transfer, he would not be able to make another move for at least five years. Although I still loved my job, I'd seen a lot of changes at the university and I wasn't sure that I wanted to be locked into another five years there. Additionally, the living situation, although better, would still not be ideal with one or both of us having a treacherous daily commute. Having weighed all the circumstances, I decided it was time for me to seriously consider the idea of moving back to Michigan.

Initially, I struggled with the idea of moving back because it felt like my ambitions were somehow moving backwards. Going "home" felt like failure. Having moved to Florida for a few years and returned to Michigan himself, Ethan understood my feelings. He helped me to reframe the situation by pointing out that while I was returning to Michigan, I wasn't going back to the same life I had left in Michigan. So many things about me and who I was in the world had changed in the years I'd spent in Georgia. This paradigm shift really helped me to see coming home as a new opportunity, a new chapter in this crazy book of Life. So after about a year and a half of contemplation, I decided it was time to make the move from Georgia back to Michigan.

Some of my apprehension had also been about the idea of finding another job that felt as important and aligned with Who I was. I was clear that the work I was doing was my Calling and I remembered the challenge of finding this position in the first place. For years colleagues who had come to the programs and trainings I led had been telling me that I could make a career of speaking and facilitating. While I loved and appreciated their support and I knew that they were right in terms of me being good at that part of my job, the idea of me creating an income based strictly on speaking engagements was hard for me to fathom. However, after multiple conversations with friends and colleagues, something in me shifted. I began to see the opportunity that they had seen for me all along. Gradually, the idea of leaving the stable, secure income of the dream job that I currently had to pursue my new dream job began to feel exciting and liberating.

The more thought and energy I gave to my dream of traveling from campus to campus to help people understand sexual and gender identity, the more the Universe provided me with clues along my journey. In the spring of 2013, shortly after I'd begun to see starting my own business as an exciting endeavor, an ad for a female business building coach came through my Facebook feed. I participated in her free online webinar and her program seemed to be exactly what I needed at that point in order to start really developing what my business would look like. It focused on identifying my niche market and developing a brand for myself.

The cost of the program was not something I could afford to pay all at once. As someone who had always lived one paycheck at a time, committing to the expense was scary for me. However, she offered a payment plan that felt manageable and after discussing it with Ethan, who always encourages me to follow my dreams and invest in myself, I committed to the program with a down payment of one third of the total cost. The day after I had taken the leap of faith and committed to the program, I found out that my state income tax refund was going to be almost the exact amount of the down payment I had committed to. I felt like that was a clear communication from the Universe that I was doing the right thing. In fact, I thanked God for such direct and clear communication that I couldn't miss it. It's amazing the kind of communication we can have with Spirit when we really pay attention.

Having committed to this program that would help me create my business, I also committed to leaving my job at Georgia and moving back to Michigan at the end of July of 2013. I submitted my letter of resignation at the beginning of May, allowing me a generous amount of time to work on building a website and some of the other foundational pieces to establishing my business while still wrapping up loose ends on campus. I was grateful for such a long period of time to process and be really present to the transition that was happening in my life.

My time in Athens and at The University of Georgia had been, and remains to be, one of the most impactful and transformative periods of my life. I was incredibly grateful for the opportunity to achieve my dreams and to live my passion. I was also very aware of the ways in which I had grown as a person and as a professional during my time there. Things certainly had not always been easy, but every challenge was a blessing as I emerged from each a more evolved and authentic version of myself. I had come to love Athens in a way one might love their hometown and was so incredibly grateful for all of the amazing people and opportunities that had surrounded me. It had certainly been a charmed experience from beginning to end and I was very intentional about saying goodbye to Athens in ways that were meaningful and took full advantage of the time I had left there. I visited all of my favorite places, made plans with all of my favorite people, did all the things that I always wanted to do but had not made the time for, and even made a point to journal about my feelings of gratitude for such an amazing chapter in my life. Even in retrospect, I get emotional thinking about what Athens and that time in my life was for me.

It seemed only fitting that my best friend, Jenny, who had lovingly ushered me into Athens also made a trip down a few days early to help me finish packing up my apartment and drive back with me and Ethan. I had lived there just about three weeks short of five years the day we turned in my keys and drove out of town. It felt so surreal to be leaving for good, especially having only a vision of what life was going to be like in the next chapter. I was entering uncharted territory as I set out to start my own business and I had no idea about the obstacles that awaited me on that journey.

FINDING GOD

CHAPTER TWENTY-SEVEN
Discovering *The Secret*

Before I moved in with Ethan, he and I made a plan. He would provide for us financially while I worked to get my business off the ground. In theory, we both understood that this was not something that would happen overnight. However, the reality of living in a home that I wasn't paying for and paying off my debts with money that wasn't mine created unease in my body. Suddenly, I noticed this obsession to make money. It did not help that the process of starting a business still felt quite overwhelming and nebulous to me.

Ethan was certainly right in his reframing of Michigan for me in that I was not returning to a place I was familiar with. Before I left for Georgia, I had lived eight years in a college town two hours north of where we were currently living. Despite having grown up there, I had no connections to anyone in the Detroit area, much less to anyone in the LGBTQ+ community. Although the idea of being my own boss sounded fantastic, the downside was that I had no network. I quickly learned the benefit of working within a system where you have a title and an office and a built-in community that values and needs your services. I had gone from being the face of an office, a symbol and leader in a community, to feeling completely invisible and disconnected.

I explored ways to get involved with the LGBTQ+ community in Detroit, but nothing felt even remotely close to the significance of the work I had been doing in Georgia. Feeling apprehensive about the idea of starting my own business, I applied for LGBTQ+ jobs for which I was seemingly perfectly qualified, in some cases even overqualified. I never heard from any of them. What I couldn't recognize at the time but see in retrospect, is that this lack of response was another example of clear communication from the Universe. It wasn't the communication I was hoping for or looking for, but it was clearly guiding me back to the path of answering my Calling. Yet, I refused to stay on the path.

I found myself in a vicious loop of feeling frustrated that I wasn't making any money, overwhelmed by the process of getting my business started, which led to me taking no action at all, which brought me back to the frustration that I wasn't making any money. It was both maddening and paralyzing at the same time. Rather than taking action - any action - of establishing my business, I would keep myself occupied with other things that I felt like I should be doing but didn't really want to be doing. Like cleaning the house. Or cooking dinner.

One day while I was looking for jobs online for Ethan's niece who we were trying to help to get on her feet, I came across a job listing for David's Bridal. Having purchased my wedding gown there, I remembered thinking when I was there for my appointment that it seemed like it would be a fun place to work. I immediately went to their website and put an application in for myself. Within a week I had gone in for an interview and managed to negotiate an hourly rate that was about three dollars above the minimum wage. Additionally, I would get a 25% employee discount which I figured might come in handy as we continued to plan our 2014 wedding.

Initially, Ethan supported my decision to apply at David's Bridal because he saw it as a healthy opportunity for me to get out of the house and interact with the rest of the world. However, he also knew that I was selling myself short by spending so much time on this part-time job. He would later gently suggest that I reassess where I'm putting my energy and consider focusing my attention on what I left my full-time dream job to pursue. I knew he was right, but I was also still dominated by my own fears and insecurities and would always find myself back in the vicious loop of frustration, overwhelm, and no action.

One day when I was feeling particularly stuck, and Ethan was over giving me pep talks, he sat me down on the couch, equipped me with a notebook and inserted a DVD into the DVD player.

"I love you. I want you to watch this and take notes. Press pause if you need to, rewind and re-watch it if you need to. But watch it. I'm going to work," he instructed me before kissing me on the forehead and heading out for the day.

The DVD he had put on was one that he'd been telling me to watch for weeks and I had not gotten around to it because, you know, I had so many other things that I needed to be doing to make money! It was *The Secret*, which is also a book by Rhonda Byrne. It is all about the Law of Attraction and manifesting all that you want to have, be, and do in your life. I was captivated. I took pages and pages of notes. watched it multiple times. It broke down the process of manifesting things into my life in a way that I had never heard before. It also talked about God in ways that made sense to me and helped me to realize that there were many different ways to talk about God that did not necessarily have to do with religion.

While the practice of manifesting made perfect sense when you understand the Law of Attraction and how it works, my skeptic brain still also questioned the effectiveness of thinking things into reality. However, this would prove to be just the beginning of my exploration of the Law of Attraction.

CHAPTER TWENTY-EIGHT
Seeing The World Through A New Lens

At some point, I learned about an app called Meetup that was designed with the intention of using technology to reconnect with people face to face. This was an app that had been very popular with people who had recently relocated to a new city and were looking to meet new people and find community. You could search groups by your interests and at some point, I came across a group called the Billionaire's Club. This was a group that met once a month to discuss the Law of Attraction. I was immediately intrigued and decided to check it out.

At the first meeting I attended, they started with a recorded guided meditation that was led by someone named Esther Hicks. At this point, I had no knowledge of Esther Hicks, but I loved the guided meditation and went home and Googled her to try and find the meditation to use at home. I'm sure it was through this Google search that I discovered Abraham Hicks. Before I knew it, we had ordered *Law of Attraction: The Basic Teachings of Abraham* in both paperback and CD formats and were listening to the CDs on repeat in our vehicles. *The Basic Teachings of Abraham* covered not only the Law of Attraction but also the Law of Deliberate

Creation and the Law of Allowing as well as some methods for implementing and leveraging these laws of the Universe to manifest everything you want in your life.

Ethan and I were immediately fascinated with Abraham Hicks. Abraham is a group of non-physical entities that Esther Hicks and her husband Jerry began channeling in the 1980's while seeking answers to Life's big questions. Their book begins with Esther and Jerry telling the story of how they met Abraham through a daily meditation practice. That story and how they were called to begin practicing meditation was intriguing itself, but the rest of the book was all channeling of Abraham, through Esther. If you're not familiar with the concept of channeling, it is described as a form of communication between humans and angelic beings, nature spirits, non-physical entities, or even animals and pets.

Now, I'm gonna stop right here and just state for the record that this whole thing was super "woo woo" for me. My academic, skeptic ego listened with a very critical ear. However, what I found was that not only did the message being delivered make perfect sense with everything I'd experienced in life to that point, but listening to the audio book gave me the opportunity to hear the authenticity of the channeling. By that I mean that there were a few observations that I made that convinced me that this wasn't just some wacky lady making crazy claims about channeling and accessing some make believe higher intelligence.

First of all, while I'd never heard life talked about in the specific terms of the Law of Attraction, Abraham gave example after example of the Law of Attraction in our day to day experiences. The concept of the Law of Attraction is rooted in the fact that everything in the Universe is Energy and all energy attracts like energy. The examples of us recognizing this in our everyday lives that Abraham shares are common proverbs like "birds of a feather flock together" and "the better it gets, the better it gets; the worse it gets, the worse it gets." As I listened, I could not refute the information that was being shared.

Additionally, as a public speaker myself, I noticed a few things about Esther's speech as she was channeling Abraham. The first was that there were virtually no stutters, false starts, or fillers in her speech, whatsoever. Each and every idea and sentence was delivered with exact and precise language that perfectly communicated the concept. However, it was also clearly not scripted or rehearsed, but rather conversational. Additionally, the channeling was originally recorded on cassette tapes. So, while I suppose it would not be impossible to edit them, there seemed to be no editing of the recordings.

The other thing that I noticed as I listened to the CD's repetitively, was that the "voice" of Abraham seemed to speak in a way that sounded incredibly dated. From the word choices to the speech pattern, Abraham sounds like a voice from a very far away time and place. Abraham would consistently put the negative at the end of the sentence instead of at the beginning like we do in modern language.

For example, instead of saying "It does not matter," they would say "It matters not." This language pattern was used consistently without exception throughout the audiobook which consisted of five CDs running five to six hours in length. There also seemed to be a hint of an English accent present throughout the recording that was not present in the first part of the first disc when Esther and Jerry are telling the story of how they met Abraham.

Familiar enough with the Law of Attraction from having watched the film *The Secret* several times, that information completely resonated with us. However, it was the Law of Deliberate Creation and, in particular, the Law of Allowing that truly blew my mind a bit.

The concept of the Law of Deliberate Creation was covered in *The Secret* as well and speaks to the idea that we are all constantly manifesting our reality whether we're aware of it or not through the energy that we are emitting into the Universe. So, the Law of Deliberate Creation is about being intentional about the things we manifest in our lives by focusing on the things we want and make us feel good as opposed to wallowing in our negative feelings about what we are unhappy with or do not want in our life. In *The Secret*, they teach the formula of manifesting as Ask + Believe = Receive. *The Basic Teachings of Abraham* speaks to this same concept. Abraham talks about the importance of balancing our "wanting," which is the Ask part of the equation, with our "belief" in order to most efficiently manifest the life we want.

to live.

Some are quick to call the Law of Deliberate Creation nonsense or sacrilegious in some way. However, the exact same concept is taught in The Bible. Christians are taught to turn to God and to pray for what they want and need in their life - the Ask part of the equation - and to have faith in God - the Belief part of the equation - that God will provide what they seek - the Receive part of the equation. The concept is exactly the same, only the story or language used is different. Christians are also taught that God is omnipotent, omniscient, and omnipresent. Similarly, the Law of Attraction is based on the fact that everything is Energy, making it omnipresent. Like God, Energy can never be destroyed nor created, making it omnipotent. It can only be transferred from one source to another, making it omniscient as it exists in everything throughout all space and time, past, present and future.

Again, having some frame of reference about the Law of Attraction and the Law of Deliberate Creation, I easily grasped these ideas and felt very connected to them based on my lived experience. The Law of Allowing, however, was a different story.

The Law of Allowing as explained by Abraham states, "I am that which I am, a changing thing indeed, and while I am that which I am, I am willing to allow all others to be that which they are." As someone whose career had consisted of teaching people about differences in order to make the world a safer place for people, this initial definition was not necessarily life shattering. However, a few pages later Abraham says, "You will know you are allower when you allow all others - *even in their unallowing of you.*" The first time I heard this, it was such an "Aha!" moment that I had to back up the CD and listen to it a few more times. Said another way, it's basically, my allowing you to be Who you are, in no way prevents me from being Who I Am. It was this clarification that changed the way I saw my work - and the world - forever.

CHAPTER TWENTY-NINE
My First Exercise in the Law of Allowing

Long before I moved back to Michigan and watched *The Secret* or had any knowledge of Abraham Hicks and the Law of Allowing, I met a fellow traveler on a flight from Atlanta to Detroit. She and I had an interaction that was a perfect real life illustration of the Law of Allowing. Having taken many flights back to Michigan over the three years I'd been living in Georgia, I'd learned to choose the window seat so that I could have a place to lean my head for a nap and successfully avoid obligatory small talk with other passengers. These well-meaning travelers would inevitably ask what I did for a living, which always led to an internal conflict about whether to speak in code or be very transparent about my work. Fortunately, my evasive tactic did not work out in this situation.

As we were settling in and preparing for take-off, a woman named Ruth was seated in the dreaded middle seat. I perceived her to be several years younger than me. She had a gentle, sweet energy about her as she sparked up a conversation with me.

"Do you live in Detroit or are you just visiting?" She asked.

"Oh, I'm visiting, but I'm originally from the area. How about you?" I replied in kind.

"I'm visiting as well. I'm on my way to a women's missionary retreat."

Noted, I thought to myself as I replied with a smile. "Nice. Where are you going for your retreat?"

"I guess it's about two hours from the airport. I don't know exactly where. I'm meeting some other women in Detroit and we're shuttling there together," she replied.

"Ah, I see," I responded as I shifted my focus out the window. After a few minutes of silence, she re-engaged me in conversation.

"So, what brings you to visit Detroit? Is your family still here?" She asked.

"I'm going to visit my boyfriend for the weekend. It is homecoming weekend at my alma mater where we met 14 years ago and so we're going back there to celebrate." I had no idea why I was giving her so much information. I wasn't trying to carry on a conversation throughout the flight.

"Oh, wow! How nice! So, you have been together for 14 years?" She asked.

That's what you get for giving too much information, I thought to myself as I prepared to share more of mine and Ethan's story. I love our story, but I wasn't trying to tell it to a stranger on a plane, especially in light of the fact that she was on her way to a women's missionary retreat and I was feeling the need to tiptoe around which details I would include.

"Oh, no, we have actually only been a couple for about five months, but we've known each other for 14 years," I succinctly replied.

Despite my best efforts to avoid getting into a deep conversation, Ruth continued to lure me in with her genuine interest and inquisitive spirit. At some point, the topic of what I did for a living, indeed, came up. Initially I played the game where I was not completely forthcoming about the specific kind of work that I did. I was still trying to avoid any kind of awkwardness that I was sure would arise if I mentioned I was queer.

"So, what do you do in Georgia?" She asked.

Here we go, I thought. "I work at The University of Georgia."

"Oh, really? What do you do there?" She asked.

"I work in student affairs," I replied in code. "How about you? What do you do?" I asked, slyly shifting the focus to her. I'd had lots of practice at this game.

"I'm an assistant girls' dean at a live-in Christian Bible school," she replied.

Oh, I am definitely not telling her what I really do, I thought.

"I live in and oversee the girls' dorm," she went on.

She seemed young to me to be an assistant dean until she explained more to me about her job, which felt a little bit like a resident hall director job on a college campus, only for high school girls. After telling me a little more about her job, she came back to try to better understand what it was that I did.

"So, do you work directly with students?" she asked.

She is not going to let this go, is she? I wondered.

"Yeah, I do." I answered, trying to leave it at that. But, as they say in the South, bless her heart, she was truly curious about the work that I did. Somehow she finally got me to tell her that I was the director of the LGBT Resource Center.

"L...B...G...T?" She struggled as most people not familiar with the community usually do.

"LGBT. Lesbian, gay, bisexual, and transgender. I teach people about gender and sexuality," I finally said.

I could see the surprise on her face and the wheels turning as, like so many others, she tried to figure out how I could possibly have gotten into this work. There was some more conversation back and forth about the specific nature of my work before she finally had to ask.

"How did you get into that work?" It was clear that it had not yet occurred to her that I might be anything other than straight.

"Well, I have a Masters in Educational Leadership, but most of what got me here was my life experience," I replied.

"So, you're gay...?" she asked, clearly confused.

"Mmm...if I have to choose a label, I prefer queer," I answered.

"Did you say 'queer'?" Again, a common response to this statement.

I affirmed that she had heard me correctly and we proceeded to have a conversation about the word "queer," it various connotations and why I choose to use if for myself. I explained to her that, like with almost all language, the use of the word "queer" is all about time, place, manner, and intent. I also explained that, while historically the word has been primarily used as a slur - and certainly continues to be used with that intention - it is also a word that has been reclaimed by those who were once oppressed by it. That being said, I acknowledged that there are still many people who do not like the word, regardless of the fact that it has been reclaimed. Some people experience attraction to a variety of people and the term "queer" allows for some flexibility that terms like "lesbian" or "gay" don't.

"But...you're in a relationship with a man?" Ruth said, still genuinely trying to understand why I would identify as queer.

"Yes, I am. And, this one relationship does not define me."

I went on to share with her that I had identified with various labels at different times in my life. I was straight until I wasn't. For some time after that, I wasn't sure what label worked best for me. My relationship pattern for several years was actually quite bisexual in that I would date a woman and then I would date a man and then I would date a woman, and so on until one final relationship with a man in which I had determined I was done with men. I'm sure most women - and some men - have been able to relate to this sentiment at some point in their lives! From that point on, I dated only women for over ten years, until Ethan showed back up in my life, at which point, I was totally confused about my label again.

I had never really identified as straight. By that, I mean my sexuality and what I call it was never part of my consciousness until I was in a relationship with a woman and was no longer "normal." Even after being in a relationship with a woman, I still wasn't sure if that made me a lesbian. This was especially true since I wasn't sure that I'd never be in a relationship with a man again. After all, it was not that I had determined I didn't like men, only that I clearly loved this particular woman in a way that was more than just platonic. I also felt some safety in maybe identifying as bisexual because, in my mind, my parents might more easily accept it because it kept the option of being with a man on the table.

During this conversation with Ruth, I introduced her to the concept of attraction versus behavior versus identity. I tried to convey how, when I determined I was done with men, I began to strongly identify with the word lesbian and did for most of my adult life. In fact, when Ethan and I began dating, I grappled with what this meant for my own identity. As a lover of language who believes that words are powerful and important, the word "lesbian" clearly no longer fit for me as I was clearly no longer *only* attracted to women. However, while I was currently in a relationship with a male-identified person, I came to understand that one's current relationship does not determine one's sexual identity. That is, my being in a relationship with a man did not change the fact that I still experience attraction to women. In the same way that marriage does not turn off one's attraction to other people, my loving a man did not suddenly turn off my attraction to women. And, regardless of who I would ever be in a relationship with, "straight" would decidedly never describe me again.

The term "bisexual" which generally indicates attraction to both men and women, still felt too binary for me. I could remember only one cisgender man in my life to whom I was truly sexually attracted. The other relationships I'd had with men were rooted more in society's expectation that I be in a relationship with a man than my genuine desire to be in one. Through the years, I found myself to be more attracted to "masculine" people regardless of what their gender identity was. There are terms that have been coined specifically to describe this type of attraction, but those identifiers just did not resonate with me in the way that "queer" does.

As we continued our conversation, I could see the wheels turning in Ruth's head. She continued to ask questions about my experience, including common questions about my relationship with my family. I shared with her the story of how my dad had reacted when he found out that I was seeing a woman and his passing shortly after. I also told her about the distance that had come between me and my closest aunt. There was a short period where there was a break in the conversation and Ruth seemed to still be soaking in all that I had shared with her. At some point, she asked me about my religious practice.

"Have you read the Bible?"

She asked this loaded question in a tone that was full of genuine curiosity as opposed to the contempt I'd experienced from others.

"No, I haven't. I'm familiar with some Scripture and how it has been interpreted by some Christians, but I cannot say that I have read the Bible, although I've made several attempts," I explained.

She nodded as she listened, but I braced myself for a hard turn toward proselytizing when Ruth explained that her church and her employer were "Bible-believing" organizations. At the time, I didn't know exactly what that meant, but in the context of this conversation I interpreted it to mean that she believed the Bible said that homosexuality is wrong and so that is what they believe. I have come to learn that the term "Bible-believing" is the belief that the Christian Bible contains no theological contradictions, historical discrepancies, or other such *errors*. So, basically, the Bible is the end all, be all and it's all absolutely true.

I offered my opinion on what that might mean for other practices that are named in the Bible as sins but we still practice regularly in the world with zero push back, like eating shellfish or pork and even handling the skin of a pig - hello Sunday night football! I also pointed out that any Scripture that might remotely be interpreted to be about homosexuality had all appeared in the Old Testament, which to me understanding, God had overruled, so to speak, with the coming of Christ establishing a new covenant of faith and love with mankind. I also took the opportunity to share with her the name of an excellent documentary called *For the Bible Tells Me So* in which several Christian families share their experience of having a child that comes out as gay and how they reconciled that information with their own faith.

This seemed to steer the conversation in a direction that was more focused on my relationship with God, which was something to which I was much more equipped to speak. Ruth seemed to focus on the message that God is with each of us and God's love is unconditional. I still felt like perhaps there was an underlying insinuation that God loving me unconditionally and wanting the best for me meant that God wanted me to turn away from this "sin," but would love me regardless. Maybe that was the case, or maybe that was my own old wounds being prodded.

What I appreciated about Ruth was that regardless of what her own beliefs about my life were, she led with love. It was clear that she was being challenged with the task of reconciling my real life experience with what she believed in her heart to be the Truth. She could have easily defaulted to preaching to me or trying to convince me that her perspective was the only perspective. Instead, she chose to focus on the things she could understand and relate to and the ways in which she might be able to inspire me to strengthen my relationship with God. She seemed to inherently understand that it was not her responsibility to single-handedly try to "save" me from myself. She understood that my relationship with God was just that, between me and God. She showed true faith in God's power by not trying to take on the task of persuading me to her way of thinking, but rather empowering me to connect directly with God and work it out on my own.

As the flight drew to an end and the plane descended, Ruth offered her prayers for me and my family. She trusted that God would lead us to find common ground and to reconnect. Once we were on the ground and we could access our carry-on luggage, she reached into her bag under the seat in front of her and she pulled out a small Bible. It was leather bound with a snap closure and it appeared to be quite worn.

"I want you to have this," she said as she handed me the Bible. Stunned and a little uncomfortable, I looked at her with confusion.

"It's my Bible. I have studied it daily for the past eight years, I take it with me everywhere I go, but I feel compelled to give it you, Jennifer."

Still overcome by the gesture, I declined the gift. It felt too personal and like such a precious possession. I couldn't imagine taking it.

"No, I can't possibly. This is your personal Bible!" I objected.

"I know. I truly want you to have it. I hope that you will find it as precious as I have over the years. I have bookmarked a special Scripture that is one of my favorite and I feel compelled to share with you."

She insisted for a few moments more and I accepted the gift.

Before getting off the plane, we exchanged contact information. I gave her one of my business cards and she wrote her email address on the back of one of my cards for me.

When I got into Ethan's truck after picking up my luggage, I told him about my experience with Ruth.

"So...this woman just gave me her Bible," I said and I proceeded to tell him the whole story.

"Well? What does the Scripture she bookmarked for you say?" he asked.

I opened the Bible to the pages where she'd left my card with her contact information on it and read the Scripture she had circled for me.

"Jeremiah 29:11. For I know the thoughts that I think toward you, saith the Lord, thoughts of peace, and not of evil, to give you an expected end," I read aloud as Validation Tears filled my eyes.

CHAPTER THIRTY
Following the Woo Woo

For more than ten years, I had been teaching people about LGBTQ identities and approaching it from a standpoint that always felt like a battle or a debate. I was so attached to the outcome of persuading people in their hearts and minds that LGBTQ people were just as valid and worthy of their approval as anyone else, that the work had become exhausting. It was as if somehow my own self-worth depended on the validation of these other people. So, the experience of accepting other people's perspectives, while standing firmly, yet compassionately in my truth was the most freeing feeling I'd had in a very long time.

For the first time, I came to understand that the issue didn't have to be this way *or* that way but that, contrary to popular belief, there is such a thing as co-existing in our difference. All we had to do was choose to make it so. Said differently, you don't have to be wrong for me to be right and vice versa. I also realized, somehow for the first time, that if I want others to allow me to be who I am...I must also allow them to be who they are, *even in their unallowing of me.* Most of us get the first part of the equation - allowing others to be who they are. However, it's that last part about allowing others - even in their unallowing of us - that I felt was the key to unlocking a whole different world.

Although it had always come a bit more naturally for Ethan anyway, we began to really practice leveraging the Law of Attraction in our life. I would use a gratitude journal and list the blessings I was grateful for each day as a method of raising my vibration. I would journal about my hopes, dreams and aspirations which was an activity in communicating with the Universe. I was placing my order, so to speak. During this time, although I recognized the parallels between the two and was beginning to perceive God and the Universe as one in the same, I found myself more inclined to use the word Universe instead of God. Perhaps that's because I was working specifically on manifesting things in my career and income producing opportunities and it felt weird to ask God for money. However, as I continued on this spiritual journey, I would come to understand that nothing in this Universe is not of God - even money. But there was also a part of me that had always struggled with the concept of everything being up to this invisible entity in the sky. The word "Universe" felt more expansive and inclusive, the way that I perceive God to be.

As we continued to listen to Abraham Hicks and to play with the Law of Attraction, the academic in me wanted more and more information. I began to read other books by the author of *The Secret*, Rhonda Byrne, and to see how the Law of Attraction was working in our current experiences as well as the ways it had been working in my life all along. One of the most profound examples of having manifested my dreams into reality through the Law of Attraction had been my position at Georgia. From the moment I left that in-service about transgender identity, I was on a mission to become a director of an LGBT Resource Center. I declared it and I moved forward with inspired action, immediately pursuing my master's degree in educational leadership. Although that degree qualified me to do lots of different types of work in higher education, my sole - or soul - intention was to become a director of an LGBT Resource Center. At some point along the way I was willing to settle for any kind of job in student affairs to be near the partner I was with at the time. However, that relationship dissolved, refocusing me on my goal of being the director of an LGBT Resource Center. Interestingly, that position led to so many other things in my life that have delivered me to where I am today, including writing this book. But it didn't start with that dream job.

If there's one thing that I will be forever grateful to my mother for, it is for raising me to believe that I can do or be anything I want if I just put my mind to it. She told me this countless times when I was growing up. While some may say that's what moms are supposed to tell you, whether they believe it or not, I feel like my mom did believe it for her kids. Whether she did or not, she convinced me that it was true! This belief worked for me because it's how the Universe functions. What we think about, we bring about. Thoughts become things. If we believe we can, we will. I feel like I've always had a pretty healthy self-esteem and have always seen myself as an achiever. I was always an outgoing, competitive kid who believed that I would be someone who made the world a better place. For the most part, I did achieve the things I put my mind to achieving. I am blessed to be able to say that it's hard for me to even remember many disappointing moments in my childhood. I understand now that my success had everything to do with believing that I could be, do, or have anything I put my mind to and having the focus to go after the things that I really wanted. For this reason, it is important that we instill this understanding in all of our kids.

In addition to recognizing the Law of Attraction at work in our lives, I could not find any evidence that contradicted it. Being the intellectual and skeptic that I was, I thought critically about the things that we were learning from Abraham. I would try to see if I could find holes in the concepts. I searched for times in my life that it didn't seem to work. However, five years later, I've yet to have an experience or observe a situation that contradicts the laws of the Universe that Abraham shares in *The Basic Teachings of Abraham*. One of the key components to the Law of Attraction is that it is quantum physics and so, like gravity, it is working all of the time whether we are aware of it, understand it, or believe in it or not. So, even when I'm not being focused and intentional, I can still recognize what I'm manifesting, either by design or by default.

Once we had popped the energetic cork on the Law of Attraction, the Universe continuously delivered the "woo woo" or Universal synchronicities, always steering me back toward my path no matter how distracted I got. I began attending an early morning networking meeting I'd found on Meetup to promote another side gig which was a health product I was peddling to make some quick income instead of focusing on my Calling. There, I met a guy who is a spiritual coach whose business is all about helping others to follow their Spiritual Calling. I had a consultation call with him in which he immediately honed in on my insecurities around money which had been the primary roadblock between me and my business. Even just during the thirty-minute call, he had really helped me to begin to explore the root of the issue and what was really going on. I committed to three months of weekly, semi-private coaching with him and another client. Through that experience, I grew in spiritual ways that I did not anticipate.

Once our three months of coaching had ended, I continued to attend a monthly mastermind group that he led that brought together a small group of entrepreneurs who were also working to build their businesses and connecting with Spirit to do so. From month to month, I would have experiences that brought me more present to the Divine energy always at work in the world. I would see the synchronicities that had always existed but I'd never noticed before. It was as if I was seeing the world through new eyes and coming to understand how I and especially others were getting what we were getting in life, both positive and not so positive.

I began to really believe that there is something to this "higher power" thing. However, I still wasn't necessarily ready to call it a "God" thing. For so many years, I'd felt so hurt by the actions of people, and especially family, who claimed their very rejection of me was in the name of God. I had countless friends who had had similar experiences. Generally speaking, the overall message in the world was that LGBTQ people were sinners, unworthy of God's love and therefore unworthy of people's respect. So, even though I was beginning to be aware of what clearly appeared to be a connection to God, I was initially skeptical of it. Gradually, my skepticism would melt away, however, I still found it hard to speak about it in terms of "God" working things out in my life, especially to friends who were queer. I didn't want to be laughed at or dismissed as selling out to a religion that didn't value all aspects of me as a person. I also worried about being perceived as foolish - or worse, being preached to - by Christians who believed that I was not worthy of God's love.

Similar to internalized homophobia, it was almost like I was experiencing this internalized unworthiness. I knew that the connection I had with God was a real and genuine thing, but it also felt like a majority of the world believed I was a abomination. So, there was also a tiny part of me that still questioned the validity of my own experience with God. It was the residual effects of the spiritual violence I had experienced over the years and continue to witness against others even today. However, over the years I have also had what felt like some majorly magical experiences. Some of them were big, others were more subtle, but all of them would make me aware of my stronger and stronger connection with God that eventually, I just could no longer deny.

CHAPTER THIRTY-ONE

A Visit With My Dad

One of the most significant "woo woo" experiences, as I've come to lovingly refer to them, that I've had that truly shifted the energy in my life was a shamanic journeying session with an energy healer. The most profound thing that I learned from Abraham Hicks was about the existence of our non-physical selves. Some call it our Soul or Spirit, others call it our Inner or Higher Self. Whatever you call it, it is the non-physical part of us that is eternal. It is in constant communication with all aspects of our environment, seen and unseen. It existed before it entered into this temporary physical body and it will continue to exist when this physical body no longer functions. Our Soul, like everything else, is Energy, which we already discussed can be neither created nor destroyed, only transformed from one state to another and it is one with everything in the Universe. It is one with God. Shamanic journeying is a way of communicating with our Inner or Spirit Self and retrieving information.

Due to the experience I'd had with my dad and the state of our relationship when he left this world, for nearly twenty years I carried around conflict and unresolved emotions about him. As I followed my heart and my Calling to live authentically in the world and to help educate others about gender and sexuality, I felt good about my life and the work was doing. However, I also harbored such sadness and grief over the perceived loss of my dad's unconditional love. Countless times I would wonder, if he was still living, would he have come to accept and love me for who I had become in the world. I wondered if he was proud of me. While my mom's side of the family had come to an unspoken understanding of my sexuality and shown nothing but love and acceptance to me and my significant others, it did not fill the void in my heart that was left when my dad died. No matter how much support I was met with by biological family or friends who would become my chosen family, I continued to carry around this victim mentality related to my dad and his rejection of me. It had become such a heavy part of my story that it had become a part of who I was. Anyone who knew me well, knew this story. I told it to everyone.

Several years ago, a friend who is an energy healer suggested a shamanic journeying session to try to resolve the unfinished business I had with my dad when he passed away. I didn't really understand exactly what shamanic journeying was at the time, but I had experienced other energy healing modalities with this friend that had been incredibly powerful despite my ever present degree of skepticism. So, I decided to give it a try. Little did I know the closure and especially the liberation this session would bring to me.

After I arrived at my friend's healing center, she took me

into a room where the session would take place. Inside the room was a massage therapy table, a salt lamp, some crystals, and the air smelled of essential oils. The walls were a dark brown color making it feel like a close, intimate, safe space. The energy in the room was palpable. In fact, I discovered after my session that my cell phone had shut itself off while I was on my journey.

I laid on the massage table where my friend gave me a pillow and a blanket. I closed my eyes and got very comfortable. There was very soft music playing in the background. She explained to me that she was going to guide me on a journey for my Higher Self to connect with my dad. The journey began with an exercise in relaxing, detaching, and letting go of the outside world. Tuning into my breath and focusing on the sound of her voice, I tried to quiet my skeptic brain that was busy planting doubtful thoughts about the legitimacy of being able to communicate with the dead.

"Imagine you are lying in a field of green. Above you is a beautiful blue sky full of large, cumulus white clouds. Let your focus be drawn into the sky, into those beautiful clouds until you feel your spirit floating among them," my journey began. "Among the clouds appears a golden scroll surrounded by a beautiful white light. Reach up and take the scroll from the cloud. Open the scroll and with your mind's eye, imprint on the scroll the message you want to send to your father. Once you have finished your message, read it aloud."

Immediately, my skeptic brain thought it was silly. I felt foolish to be talking to my dead father as if I was somehow going to get the answers I'd been longing for. At the same time, I did not want to disrespect the work of my friend and so I pushed myself out of my comfort zone and proceeded with the exercise. There was such a vulnerability in speaking the words in the presence of someone else.

"I'm sorry, Dad. I'm sorry I disappointed you. I never meant to hurt you. All I ever wanted was to make you proud," I read from the imaginary scroll.

"Now, roll up the scroll and place it back in the brilliant white light of the cloud. Relax, breathe, and release your message to your dad and know that he has received it," my journey continued. A few minutes passed and then we continued, "Reach for the scroll again. Open the scroll and inside you will see a message from your father. Read what's on the scroll aloud."

Immediately my skeptic brain was like, *How am I supposed to know what's on the scroll?!? I don't have the woo woo powers! That's what I came for!* and I started to panic a little bit about not knowing what to say. As I laid there in silence, trying to figure it out, my skeptic brain settled down a little bit and then was like, *Ohhhh...so you just get to tell yourself whatever you need to hear. What's so magical about this?* Recognizing that my conscious brain was trying to take over, I tried to relax some more and connect with the feelings I imagined my dad would have if he were to really hear me say these words.

"I forgive you. I know you didn't mean to hurt me," I said, at first feeling like the words were coming from my brain, but also feeling the tears well up in my eyes as I spoke.

After a few moments of silence, my friend continued, "When you're done reading the scroll, simply blow on the scroll and watch the words fly away like dust. When you're ready, with your mind's eye imprint on the scroll what you want your dad to know. Once you have finished, read it aloud."

This prompt brought so much emotion. My skeptic brain had finally retreated and it felt like such a huge opportunity. It felt so important to say whatever I had needed him to hear all these years. As I laid on the table, answering the question in my mind, I could feel the emotions bubbling up inside of me.

"You hurt my feelings so much. The things that you said to me were so painful. All I wanted was for you to love me. It felt like you didn't love me anymore and it hurt so bad," I read from the imaginary scroll, full-on ugly crying at this point.

She instructed me to place the scroll back in the cloud as I had done before and reminded me to relax and breathe as I released this second message I'd sent to my dad. After a few minutes, she guided me to reach for the scroll and again and read the message that appeared inside from my father. At this point my skeptic brain was completely shut down and the messages coming through felt Divine.

"I'm sorry. I know that I hurt you. I thought that I was

doing right by you. I only wanted the best for you and I didn't know how else to protect you," I read from the imaginary scroll from my dad, tears still streaming down my face. After taking the words in, I blew on the scroll and watched the words fly away like dust as instructed.

Finally, my friend prompted me to imprint the scroll one last time, this time with a question I want to ask my dad. Again, the emotions bubbled up as the question immediately came into my consciousness.

"Are you proud of me?" I asked aloud before I could even envision the words on the scroll.

I pulled the scroll from the brilliant white cloud again and read my dad's response.

"I love you. I am proud of you. I've always been proud of you," I tearfully read from the imaginary scroll.

After allowing me a few moments to soak in the whole experience, my friend guided me out of the clouds and back to the room where she then left me in private to relax, breathe, and release anything that no longer served me.

As I left the room, I felt as if a huge weight had been lifted from me. I felt almost immediately disconnected from the experience I'd just had and especially from the negative emotions about my dad that I had carried around with me for nearly two decades. There have still been points in which my skeptic brain has snuck back in to try to convince me that it was just a simple game of me telling myself what I needed to hear. However, I also know that we are each equipped with a emotional guidance system called intuition that will not allow us to feel good about something that is not for our highest good - no matter how hard the brain tries to convince the Spirit. Our Higher Self works for our Highest Good and if something doesn't feel right, it's not. So, while my brain was trying to convince me that this was some pretend game that wasn't real, my Spirit felt differently, and I've learned that my Spirit is never wrong.

CHAPTER THIRTY-TWO
Divine Guidance

Throughout my journey, I have become more and more attuned to my connection with Spirit. During the last few years in particular, I have consistently and sometimes not so gently, been nudged back in the direction of my Calling by various hints from the Universe. Interestingly, as I follow these Divine clues, it seems my Calling continues to subtly evolve. However, one woo woo experience that I had a couple years ago, truly threw me a hard curve that I continue to discover the impacts of even now.

It was August of 2016 and we were vacationing in Venice, Florida. One morning we were at the local farmer's market when we stumbled upon a shop called The Power of One. It was the local new age store, carrying crystals, candles, essential oils, and lots of new age and spiritual books. They also had a couple of intuitives there giving readings. It happened to be Ethan's birthday and so when we discovered they were doing readings, I encouraged him to get one. He decided to do so and had an incredible reading with this woman. He said everything she said about him was impossibly accurate as far as what was currently happening in his life and even with our relationship. The most impressive thing that she knew about him was that he did not have any kids. This was impressive to me because, given our age and that he was wearing a wedding band, it would have been easy to even subconsciously assumed he was a father. In fact, she mentioned that she even second-guessed herself because it's very rare that she meets clients who don't have kids. He left feeling very excited and hopeful based on the things that she relayed to him.

Still in a bit of a rut in terms of trying to get my business off the ground, and impressed with this woman's accuracy and sensitivity, I grew curious about what she might be able to tell me. So, on our last day in town, we went back to see her so that I could get a reading. We made a point of not going in together, as we did not want the intuitive to know that I was his wife and thus have some kind of insight from the reading she'd done with him a few days before. That was my skeptic brain diligently at work, as usual.

As I was shuffling the deck of angel cards as she instructed me to do right away, she said to me, "Your angels what you to know that Love and Forgiveness is your endgame."

"Hm...what does that mean?" I asked.

"It means that's what you came for. You came into this specific physical life experience to master love and forgiveness."

Her message did not initially resonate with me. However, as she laid the cards out and then read them one by one, she shared with me her insights and, like with Ethan's reading, almost everything made perfect sense to me. When she read the card related to family, she mentioned right away something about someone having hurt me and needing to completely release the emotions attached to that. She knew that I was with my Soul Mate. Eventually, as she did with Ethan, a look of confusion came over her face as she said, "No kids…" in a tone that was definitely initially a question to herself. However, before I could affirm her statement, it was clear to her that she was correct and she knew why, immediately adding, "on purpose. No, you don't have time for kids...by that I mean, you are too much in your head for that, you have too much internal processing you're constantly doing, you would be exhausted."

This statement was incredibly profound as the decision to not have children was one that Ethan and I discussed at great length before we got married and had been a very deliberate choice that we'd come to together. However, the reason it had been such an intentional conversation between us is because, unlike Ethan, I was pretty sure that I didn't want to have kids long before he and I ever ended up together. So, it was also a pivotal conversation in our relationship, because if we didn't land in the same place about it, I knew we wouldn't make it. Despite the fact that we did end up coming to the same conclusion, for a long time I had struggled with guilt or shame about not wanting children. But I also knew in my heart of hearts that being a biological

mother was not Who I came to Be. Hearing this from thi
stranger simultaneously validated this for me while also
legitimizing her connection with Spirit as there was no wa
she could have guessed this about me.

When she talked about my relationship with Ethan, she
mentioned that he was my Soul Mate and that we had a long
history with each other, as in beyond this physical lifetime.

"He knew you and knew your endgame was love and
forgiveness and he said 'I'll help!'" She said raising her hand
in the gesture of volunteering as she explained. "So did thi
person over here," she said as she referred back to the care
that was related to a family member who had hurt me
Sensing the confusion from the look on my face, she went on
to explain. "We come into our life experience with certai
soul contracts. This person over here who hurt you, knew
your endgame of love and forgiveness and had a sou
contract with you to help you master love and forgiveness
during this lifetime. Sometimes lessons, especially that lesson
require some pain and conflict. That person offered to com
into this life experience with you to help you achieve you
endgame."

In that moment, it was as if I felt this visceral shift in m
understanding of the Universe, like I'd suddenly seer
something that could never be unseen. It had never occurred
to me that the reason someone in my life might be so difficu
is because they came into this life experience with th
agreement that they would provide me with a specifi

experience. She had seemingly unlocked a whole new room in my Spiritual house. Seeing that it was a new and profound concept for me, she wrote down the name of a short parable that she suggested I look up that would help me better understand.

"It's called *The Little Soul and The Sun*," she said as she wrote the name of it on the back of her business card, "and it's by that guy...oh, shoot...his name is escaping me now but he wrote the *Conversations with God* books."

She went on with the reading and she got to the career card, which was what I was most interested to hear about since I'd yet to have successfully launched my business.

"I'm not seeing a job...do you have a job?" She asked, a bit puzzled.

I was a bit puzzled myself about how to answer the question. While I had been working part-time at David's Bridal, I had also given them my two-week's notice before we left for vacation. I also sensed that this card was about career as opposed to a job and so the simple answer to that question in that moment was technically, no.

"Well...I've been working on starting a business," I said hesitantly, still not wanting to give her too much information that could influence her reading.

"Ah...what kind of business?" She asked.

"It's a speaking and consulting business," I replied.

"How's that going?" She asked.

"Well, I'm working on a book..." I began, referring to

another project I'd started working on three years earlier and had just recommitted to earlier in the summer. I had invested in a self-publishing program that was supposed to help me write an Amazon bestseller in 90-days. Before I could say any more than that, she interrupted me.

"It just doesn't feel like you're having fun. The energy I'm getting connected to that just feels very heavy and structured and like 'ugh.' What you're doing should feel fun, light, and full of life. It should not feel so heavy. You have to find a way to make it fun. Are you too far in to scrap it and start over?"

My heart sank. *Seriously?*, I thought. I had just spent a significant amount of money on this self-publishing program and had recommitted to writing an LGBT 101 guide of sorts but had admittedly gotten stalled in the process because of precisely what she had stated. It felt redundant, basic, and easily critiqued for being either too simple or too complicated, depending on who you ask. Eventually, I did end up abandoning that project, but not at her recommendation. In fact, it is only as I am writing this book that I am remembering this part of the conversation and realizing that I essentially did "scrap it and start over."

I left the session feeling intrigued about the reading and while there were some big immediate takeaways, like learning about the soul contracts, it was only recently that I was able to see that in some ways, that reading is where my journey to this book began. Although she had instructed me to read the parable, *The Little Soul and The Sun*, I did not immediately search for the book. A few weeks after returning home from our trip, the Universe brought it to me, anyway. A friend on Facebook posted something about the idea of forgiveness being a gift to oneself. I commented in agreement and then someone else shared a link to the story of *The Little Soul and The Sun!* I couldn't believe it. I had never heard of this story in my life and now I had heard of it twice in less than a month and the second time provided the link to actually read the parable. It was there that I learned the name of the author, Neale Donald Walsch.

Just a few weeks after that I was in my favorite bookstore, Crazy Wisdom in Ann Arbor, after having attended the monthly spiritual mastermind meeting. I was perusing aimlessly when I came across *A Course In Miracles*. I picked it up with curiosity as I'd heard it talked about in so many different circles of friends. As I was contemplating whether I wanted to take it home with me, I glanced up and noticed the book right next to it was *Conversations with God*, by Neale Donald Walsch. Seeing his name, I paused and read the title of the book again. That is when it dawned on me that this was the same book that the intuitive I'd seen several weeks before had mentioned when telling me about *The Little Soul and The Sun*. I picked it up and began reading the introduction. Even as I initially looked through the pages, I had a very clear understanding that I was supposed to read this book.

In the introduction, the author explains how the book came to be, and it's probably a hard sell for most people in our country because it's also essentially a channeled book. He explains that one day in his overwhelm and frustration with life, he sat down to write a letter to God. Shortly after putting his pen down, he heard an answer and he wrote it down and this began his conversations with God, hence the name of the book. While I would imagine that many might call him crazy or call his work blasphemous - which he acknowledges himself - I found myself intrigued and couldn't wait to read the rest of the book.

CHAPTER THIRTY-THREE

God Magic

As part of my Spiritual Journey and an attempt to establish some kind of routine for working from home, I implemented a schedule of getting up and going to the local coffee house each day where I would spend some time reading, journaling and then working on the book project. I read a chapter a day in *Conversations with God* for several weeks and it was blowing my mind in terms of completely resonating with my Soul. There was validation of things I had always understood on a subconscious level but had never heard spoken even at my own more inclusive church. There were also nuggets of Truth that opened my eyes to the obstacles I had let keep me from connecting with God in a way that felt authentic.

One of the most life-changing truths that I got from this book is that we each have a direct connection with the Divine and the opportunity to have our very own unique experience with God. Most of us are raised in religious traditions where we are told, by other humans, about what God wants and expects from us. We are told how we're supposed to interact with God as if there is only one way when, in reality, there are as many ways as there are humans. We are told what God will and will not do for us and how that will look. We are so indoctrinated with these instructions about how to be with God, that when we do have a Divine experience we don't always recognize it or we don't believe it to be a real experience because it doesn't look like anything we've been conditioned to seek.

This was incredibly freeing to me because I was able to realize that experiences that felt Divine to me, indeed were regardless of what others might think or say about them. There was something so liberating about knowing that didn't need anyone else to tell me how to connect with God or to connect with God on my behalf or even interpret my connection with God. I began to realize that not only was my connection to God direct, but it was constant. I didn't have to wait until Sunday morning to feel that connection. I didn't have to even necessarily perform any kind of formal ritual such as kneeling to pray, but rather, I could talk to God like talk to anyone else and more importantly God will respond.

I also began to realize that life is a constant manifestation of God, co-created by our human selves and our Higher Selves. Many people talk about God as an all-knowing force in the sky that controls everything that happens in the world good and bad. This is a cop-out. This concept relieves humans of any responsibility for both making positive things happen and preventing negative things from happening. have come to understand that God created humans in order to experience the magnificence of this Universe *through* us and as such, we are God's hands and feet. We have the Power within us to create not only the life that we desire, but a whole new world that is free from all pain and suffering...but first we must wake up to that Power.

One night about a year ago, Ethan and I were having one of the many versions of the conversation in which he was trying to remind me of the Power I have within myself. I say he was "trying" because, although he'd given me this pep talk what seemed like a million times to him, I'm sure, I had continued to live in this place of fear and failed to reconnect with that Power. He reminded me of all of the things I'd accomplished in my life so far and all of the resources that presented themselves to me along the way whenever I felt inadequate or like I couldn't do it alone. I was reminded again that God has always provided for me. That even when things felt hard or lonely or scary, things always worked out for my Highest Good. With this pep talk, of course came my Validation Tears as I heard him speak Divine Wisdom to me. He suggested I take some time to really reflect and be grateful for all of the ways life has worked out for me, in hopes of reconnecting me with that understanding and empowering me to take productive action with my business.

Ethan went to bed and I went into our Zen Room, which is a space in our home that we have prepared where we can be still, meditate, and connect with Spirit. I went to our meditation altar, and I got on my knees - which I don't often do - and still weeping, I began quietly talking to God. I was thanking him for all that He had done in my life. I was specifically thanking him for my experience in Athens which had always felt like such a Divine journey. I had always felt like it was exactly where I was supposed to be and what I was in the world to do. I thanked God for always making the way clear and for providing angels on Earth who have loved me and helped me along the way; for putting all the right people and opportunities along my path, for helping me to help others and for always providing exactly what I need, whether I realize it at the time or not. As I was praying and giving thanks it was as if God interrupted me, completely stopped my train of thought, and clear as a bell I received the message: *You did that.* It was so abrupt that my eyes popped open and a little startled, I found myself thinking, *What?* It was in that instant that I had this moment of clarity in which I understood that God is not some separate entity from me that works magic for people, but rather God is *in* me. I am of God and *I* have taken care of me. All of the times that life has worked out so well for me - and not so well - were not because God worked some magic, but because *I* worked my God Magic. I immediately understood that God is us and we are God, and as such, *loving ourselves is loving God.* I also realize that *only* I - through my connection with Spirit - can change my life. We *each* have the Power to make all our dreams come true.

While this was my first clear message directly from God, it would not be my last.

CHAPTER THIRTY-FOUR
Hot Pink Rubber Ball

On New Year's Eve of 2016, I decided to ring in the new year in meditation. I was still struggling with feeling frustrated with my continued failure to get out of my own way and really launch a successful business. I had been back in Michigan for more than three years and still had not replaced the income I gave up when I left Georgia. I was determined that 2017 had to be different. I had always heard that whatever you're doing on New Year's Day is a indication of how you'll spend your year. Having received the message from countless sources and directions, including the intuitive I had seen while we were on vacation in Florida earlier that year, I was determined to create a new habit of daily meditation. Ethan was scheduled to work that night and so it was a perfect opportunity to connect with Spirit as the new year arrived.

I did a YouTube search for New Year meditations and came across a 25-minute guided meditation called "The Golden Path." Around 11:45 pm, I got situated at our meditation altar in our zen room. I lit some candles, turned on the small meditation fountain, and lit some moldavite incense which is made from a tektite that is said to have metaphysical powers to accelerate emotional and spiritual evolution. My vision board for 2017 that I had created with some friends in preparation for the new year hung above the altar. It included images that represented meditation, spiritual alignment, becoming an author, financial abundance, yoga and other wellness practices. I sat on the floor, legs folded in front of me, with my phone which was cued up to the guided meditation. I put my earbuds in, closed my eyes, and focused on my breathing as I listened to the guided meditation.

The soothing male voice led me on a walk down a Golden Path through a beautiful countryside which led me to an open field along a river. There, was a small table and two chairs where I sat down to enjoy the view. Off in the distance was my Creative Self, walking toward me. She was me, but an ethereal version of me. She was vibrant and warm and her hair was the color of the Universe, blues, pinks, and purple and it somehow shined as if there were even stars in there somewhere. She sat with me for a few moments and I was instructed to agree on a tangible object she would help to manifest into my physical experience over the next few days. The object would essentially serve as proof that my Creative Self is at work within my experience of my everyday life.

Initially, my human brain tried to the get in the way as I thought too hard about the right object to choose. It felt like such an important decision that it be just the right thing. The first thing that came to mind was money, which I realized was my fear and scarcity mind speaking. Immediately, I felt like that wasn't specific enough. It had to be something I couldn't mistake for coincidence. Then, randomly, *hot pink rubber ball* popped into my mind. Hot pink rubber ball. I focused on it in my mind's eye, visualizing the color and size of the ball as instructed by the narrator that was leading me on this meditation. Having received my message, without speaking a word my stunning Creative Self got up and leisurely walked back in the direction from which she came along the river until I could no longer see her. I was guided back to the Golden Path and gradually back into my body before the meditation ended. Feeling good about having rung in the New Year doing something positive for myself, I put out the candles and the incense and headed to bed.

The next night, sticking to the intention of creating a new meditation habit, I went to our altar and listened to the meditation again. This time, as often happens when I sit down to meditate, I fell asleep before I even got to the part where I was to choose a tangible object to manifest with my Creative Self. I woke up on the zen room floor in the candlelight with silence in my earbuds. Although I felt a little discouraged that I fell asleep, I also felt accomplished that I had at least sat down and followed through on my intention. I remembered my intention of the *hot pink rubber ball* from the night before and smiled as I wondered where that would present itself.

The next day I was in a funk, and whining to Ethan about feeling stuck and overwhelmed and uninspired by the educational LGBTQ book I was supposed to be working on.

"Can you do me a favor today?" He asked as he prepared his lunch to take to work.

"What?" I asked, sensing that he was about to ask me to do something for myself.

"Will you get out of the house?" He asked. I shifted my focus away from him. I didn't feel like getting out of the house. It was January in Michigan, cold, dreary, and I had no desire to leave the comfort of our home. "Even if it's just to go to the store or whatever, just please get out of the house today."

Despite my desire to stay where I was comfortable, I agreed that I would go somewhere, anywhere, to get out of the house. Later that afternoon, I headed out to Target with my list of household items we needed. On the list was some hair product that Ethan had initially purchased for me in trial size. I ended up loving it and so I was trying to find the full size product. As I spotted what I was looking for, I slowly turned down that aisle and focused more intently on the item, making sure it was indeed the same thing Ethan had brought me. I bent over to pick up the bottle and get a closer look. As I stood back up, I noticed something out of the corner of my eye. I glanced at it and did an immediate double-take.

On this shelf that was otherwise full of wall-to-wall hair supplies, immediately to the left and just above the shelf the product I came for was on, was an empty space. In that empty space was one, lone, *hot pink rubber ball.*

That's a hot pink rubber ball, I thought, as I stood in stunned silence, my mouth literally hanging open. My eyes got big as I slowly began to realize this was the hot pink rubber ball that I shared with my Creative Self during the Golden Path meditation. I looked around searching for someone else to witness what I was experiencing, but there was no one else around. I pulled out my phone to take a photo of this ball because I could not believe it and knew that others would not believe this story. I stood there for a few more moments, feeling like I almost didn't want to move on from it and still in disbelief. I picked up the item I came for and finally moved on down the aisle, literally giggling to myself at what had just happened. After circling to the next aisle, I knew I couldn't leave the store without it and so I circled back and picked it up.

I returned home that night buzzing with excitement and connection and I couldn't wait to share the story with my friends. I did a Facebook Live video that evening from my business page and explained how this experience of manifesting the hot pink rubber ball had opened my eyes to just how powerful we are when it comes to setting an intention and then taking inspired action to manifest our dreams. While we cannot simply "think things into existence," when we set an intention the Universe will conspire with us to manifest that intention by providing clues, guidance, and opportunity. By taking inspired action, we can manifest precisely what we intend or desire for our lives. In this instance, it was guidance that came through Ethan encouraging me to get out of the house, but I had to decide to take that action. Had I simply stayed at home in my funk, would not have found that ball that night.

Life is much the same way. When we set an intention for what we want and let it go rather than focusing on or clinging to the fact that we don't have it, the Universe will immediately begin to pave the way to that intention. Then we have to be open to that suggestion or guidance and take inspired action which will inevitably lead to things our heart desires.

This hot pink rubber ball experience gave me a renewed sense of purpose and direction for the work I was to be doing in the world. It helped to remind me that we are all powerful and if I can manifest a hot pink rubber ball in matter of days, I can accomplish just about anything through this connection with the Divine. It helped me to see the world and all of the stressful and negative things that were happening through the lens of leveraging the power of the Universe to make positive change. Little did I know, this was just the beginning of the Universe showing me my Divine connection and the power that comes with it.

CHAPTER THIRTY-FIVE
The Power of Now

Still abuzz with excitement about what my meditation experience had taught me around the new year, in February of 2017, I committed to a daily gratitude practice called *The Power* by Rhonda Byrne, the same author who wrote *The Secret*. According to the Law of Attraction, gratitude is a key piece of manifesting what you desire in your life because it helps to raise your vibration. *The Power* is a 28-day gratitude practice that focuses on a different aspect of life for which to be grateful each day and an activity for expressing that gratitude. As my birthday month, I made my gratitude practice a gift to myself.

During this month of gratitude, I gradually began to see things begin to manifest in my life. From something as mundane as a baby gate that would fit our oddly-shaped landing to help keep our kitties from coming upstairs, which I'd been searching for four months, to a $100 winning PowerBall ticket, evidence of my power to co-create with my Creative Self was showing up in my life regularly.

I was still struggling a bit to figure out how to create some income with my business. I also continued to struggle with fear and anxiety about our finances and guilt about not contributing enough. However, it was tax season and so I was anticipating a tax return that would help to keep us financially comfortable for a few more months as I continued to figure it all out. We had purchased our first home in 2016 and had heard from everyone about what a great tax break it was and was banking on having a refund that was larger than usual.

Around the third week of February I received an email from our tax professional about our 2016 tax return. Not only would we not be receiving a tax refund this year, but for the first time ever, due to various circumstances we actually owed nearly $3,000 in taxes. That familiar feeling of anxiety flooded into my body. My stomach dropped, my heart pounded and my body tingled as the reaction dissipated through my body. I cried as I began to crunch the numbers and confirmed what I already knew which was that we did not have an extra $3,000. As I tried to work it out, I realized that if we paid the $3,000 by the standard IRS deadline, based on our current income, we would not be able pay our mortgage by the end of May. All of the fear, anxiety, and guilt I'd been experiencing since I moved to Michigan was now exponentially magnified and practically consuming me especially the guilt.

I knew that I could not immediately tell Ethan the news. Not having made any respectable income to speak of, I felt personally responsible for our current situation. I also knew that Ethan was doing everything he could currently do to support us, including working overtime every time the opportunity presented itself. So, telling him about the situation could only stress him out because he would be aware of a problem that he really had no power to resolve for us. I was fully aware that the only thing that could help this situation was more income and I was the only one able to create that. Incidentally, just a week earlier I had agreed to go back to David's Bridal part-time for their busy season.

For about a week I kept this information to myself, obsessing over our finances, calculating how much money I would need to bring in and how many hours I would need to work at David's Bridal to do so. I would cry myself to sleep, praying that God would help me to figure it out. I was determined that I could not tell Ethan about the situation until I had a plan or a solution. I also didn't want to tell him until his weekend because I didn't want him to be stressing about it while he was working. Aware of my inability to lie and hide things, I avoided contact with Ethan as much as possible by rising early and going to the local coffee house to "work" aka, obsess over our situation and figure out a solution, before he woke up.

On day six of freaking out, I woke up with an overwhelming feeling of fear. My heart was racing, my stomach churning. I tried to stay in bed and breathe to calm my heart but my stomach was convincing me to put my feet on the ground and make my way to the bathroom. It was not pretty. After taking care of that business, I took a moment in our zen room to get on my knees and pray for God to calm my heart as I focused on my breathing and centered myself. This brought enough relief for me to get up and get dressed to head out to the coffee house and try to take some productive action.

For literally years now, I had been in this state of paralysis by analysis with my business. Overwhelmed with the thoughts of what I should do, for far too long, I had done nothing. Now, I was in a place of true desperation and willing to do anything to jumpstart my business. As I drove I began making a mental list of the action I was going to take when I got to the coffee house. I listed out loud to myself the contacts I was going to make with people at local LGBTQ organizations to initiate some conversation about how I could best serve their organization.

As I began declaring my plans out loud to myself, it felt as if God was speaking directly into my right ear, like a kid in the backseat, "That's right, Jennifer. You just keep putting one foot in front of the other. You don't know what the end of the month looks like, or what next week looks like. Just keep putting one foot in front of the other and doing what you said you were going to do." Suddenly, I understood that the power is in *this* moment. That I must stop worrying about whether the money will show up a month from now so we can pay our bills because while I'm doing that, I'm losing *the* moment to change the outcome and simply expediting myself to the end of the month where the money is not there. I was reminded that God is literally within me and that the

Universe will provide all the guidance I need to get to where I am going and to be Who I came into this world to Be.

Validation Tears streamed down my face as this message came through to me clear as day and I cried the rest of the way to the coffee house. As I pulled up to my destination a calmness washed over my whole body. It was a familiar feeling, similar to the peacefulness that came when I had prayed for God to calm my heart the morning I was moving to Georgia. I got out of my car and for the first time in a week, I felt light and at ease and knew everything was going to be alright. Fortunately, this experience would turn out to be a permanent shift in my energy around money and finances.

When I got inside, I sat down to do some journaling about what had just transpired between me and God. I pulled up YouTube to play some root chakra meditation music and I received another strong message. After that whole conversation we'd just had about being Who I Am and taking inspired, guided action and trusting that God is with me every step of the way, the ad on the YouTube video was from the Isha Foundation and was all about the importance of raising human consciousness to save our planet and society from its destruction. This was something I'd been exploring for quite some time and the synchronicity of the interaction with God and then the affirmation of the message just felt so powerful. In that moment, it was a clear message to me that God was saying, "By the way, this is the thing you're supposed to be talking about."

That evening, after Ethan had gone to work, I sat down again with our finances and came up with a solid plan for paying our taxes. It was going to be uncomfortable for a few months for both Ethan who hates to feel restricted by anything and for me who would need to be working as much as possible to make ends meet, but ultimately, it was feasible. The next morning, feeling better that I had a solution to the problem, I finally shared the situation with Ethan. Thankfully, he is so Divinely connected that as soon as I began to explain what had happened, he immediately knew in his Spirit that this situation was mine and that he did not need to get wrapped up in any of the emotion or stress of it. The conversation was so calm and connected. It also helped me to feel closer to him than I had in a long time. I realized that I had isolated myself in fear.

That night, I went to a program at a local LGBTQ organization and introduced myself to two different leaders in the community. One of those conversations was full of good energy and eventually led to a consulting contract with a local LGBTQ rights organization. Although it took about six weeks to get to that point, ultimately that opportunity provided significant income for me in the year to follow. In the meantime, a family member that we had confided in about the taxes we owed insisted on giving us the money to pay them. This was yet another experience in which the Universe continued to teach me that it's always conspiring in our favor...and that I was to tell the world about it.

CHAPTER THIRTY-SIX
Who I Really Am

I have come to realize that I am called to be a Light in the world for people who are seeking a connection with Spirit but think they are somehow unworthy. I had to go on my own journey in order to help others on theirs. Although the part of my journey in which I lost my dad was incredibly difficult, I also believe it was Divinely orchestrated. It took me more than twenty years to figure it out, but eventually, I realized that were it not for him drawing that clear line in the sand and declaring my unworthiness of God's love with such conviction, I don't know that I would have necessarily discovered my own connection to the Divine. Like some kind of reverse psychology, it was as if his denying me of it, caused my heart to become more focused on a Spiritual connection than it had ever been. I fully believe he had to say those hurtful things in order for me to end up on this Journey.

It is also clear to me that there have been so many other people Divinely placed in my experience to ensure that I discovered Who I Am and that I accomplish the work that I came into this life to do. For example, the intuitive in Venice, Florida who introduced me to the concept of soul contracts.

When she first talked during my reading about someone in my family having hurt me and my needing to completely release the emotions around that, ironically, my dad was no who came to mind. In fact, it wasn't until I was in the thick of writing this book that I had the realization that the act of doing so was the total releasing of the emotions around the hurt my dad had caused.

The writing of this story has been the act of fully forgiving my dad and acknowledging the way in which he loved me. As crazy as it may sound, I gained an appreciation for the way that he treated me so many years ago. After nearly two decades of feeling victimized and hurt by him, I suddenly recognized that I wasn't a victim at all. My dad loved me so much that he agreed to come into this life experience with me and do whatever was necessary to ensure that I achieved the experience of mastering Love and Forgiveness. What better way to master Love and Forgiveness than to overcome rejection by a person who is supposed to love you unconditionally? Like the Friendly Soul in the parable, *The Little Soul and The Sun*, I believe my dad was "pretending so hard" that he forgot himself. He was willing to say terrible hurtful things to me - which never feel good to the person saying them, either. His words helped me to remember Who I Really Am, to examine my own Spirit, and seek the Truth. I am forever grateful that the Spiritual Journey he led me to allowed me to also eventually remember Who *He* Really Is through the writing of this book.

It has also led me to understand that the realization of Who I Really Am is a direct product of my sexuality. It was my love for another woman that instigated the whole hurtful experience with my dad that ultimately set me on my Spiritual Journey to discovering Who I Really Am and what I came to do and Be in the world through my love for other people. So while the label of "queer" is a societal term with regard to who we love, I know that it is absolutely Divine that my Spirit is so open to loving others, regardless of how they identify.

I know that I am Divinely Queer.

ACKNOWLEDGMENTS

Feeling gratitude and not expressing it is like wrapping
a present and not giving it.
William Arthur Ward

I am of the belief that every moment of my life has led me to this one. That belief makes writing this part of the book incredibly challenging. There have been so many people along my Journey that I am convinced God placed in just the right time, place, and role in my life to ensure I delivered this message to the world. I mentioned several of them in the telling of my story, some by name, some by description. However, there are also many others who have touched my life in significant ways who do not show up in the telling of my story. Perhaps someday there will be other books that reveal other aspects of my life in which those people do make an appearance, but in the meantime, I want to acknowledge their presence on my Journey and my gratitude for their influence in my life, big or small.

A common experience among queer people is that we often lose our close relationships with our biological family members when we come out about who we are. As I share in my story, I was no exception, particularly on my dad's side of the family. However, my mom's side of the family - which is quite extensive given that my mom had five sisters and they all have kids who have kids - almost collectively have never made an issue of my identity. Rather, they have embraced me and my partners and always treated me with the same love and respect they showed to anyone else in the family. In fact every last one of my aunts and many of their kids attended our wedding in 2014 and that meant the world to me. We don't all get together nearly enough and I would be remiss if I didn't take this opportunity to openly express my gratitude for their love and acceptance.

Despite the distance between me and my dad's siblings, have been fortunate to have reconnected with a few of my cousins as an adult and that connection has been a blessing. Jason, Brandi, and I are all close in age and so we share similar memories of our family together. Despite being raised by parents who seemed to share my dad's perspective about sexuality and really, life in general, both Jason and Brandi hold values similar to mine. It has been such a gift, after years of feeling estranged from that part of my family, to have rekindled our relationship and for them to share with me memories they have of my dad and of our family before came out. They have also allowed me over the years to process my feelings about my relationship with other members of my dad's family and to offer me comfort and validation.

I have also been incredibly blessed throughout my life to have cultivated a group of people I affectionately call my family of choice. Some of them I've known since junior high school, others I encountered along my way, but all of them have shown me absolutely unconditional love and support through some of the most challenging and most joyful times of my life.

My oldest and dearest friend, Jenny Albee is like a sister to me. She has laughed with me and cried with me and loved me like no else in my life. She, too, has a gift with words and has been a voice of encouragement and support for me at every turn. Jenny has helped me make some of the best decisions of my life and has loved me through all of the not-so-great choices I've made without so much as a hint of "I told you so." She has been one of the few people in my life with whom I know I can share anything without shame and I know that she will hold space for me and that alone has been a priceless gift. She has honored me with the responsibility of serving as her first-born's Godmother and words cannot express the love, affection, and gratitude I have for her and her family.

Another member of my chosen family is Tony Bommarito. Tony was my first boyfriend and has become my forever friend. Regardless of the time and space that has separated us over the years, we have always picked up right where we left off and loved each other like family. Tony was actually the first person to ever suggest I write a book. For years, as I would share with him the drama of the moment about who I was dating, or where I was moving, or what my family thought about it, he would always reply with, "when are you going to write a book?" or, "you really need to come up with a name for your life, because it's like a soap opera." I was always amused by this suggestion and insisted he was the only one who would be interested in reading it. However, I have no doubt that Spirit worked through our conversations to continuously direct me on the path to authorship. I am eternally grateful for his friendship, especially on the days that we bicker like brother and sister, and I hope that he finds this long-awaited book satisfying.

Dr. Jon Humiston is another friend that I consider to be a member of my chosen family. Having met during my time working at Central Michigan University under less than ideal circumstances - I was reporting an incident of harassment to his office - incidentally, we became fast friends. In addition to doing work with the Office of Gay & Lesbian programs and the Association of Lesbian & Gay Faculty & Staff, we eventually would have lots of classes together as we both pursued our Master of Arts in educational leadership. We spent hours upon hours processing inevitable work drama and learning so much about each other along the way. He was always in my corner in every way. We were BFFs and, to this day, I honestly believe that had it not been for Jon urging me to follow up with The University of Georgia about my application for the position in the LGBT Resource Center that my life could look very different. Had I missed that opportunity, there's a good possibility that Ethan and I may not have crossed paths a third time and who knows where I might be, today? I am eternally grateful for Jon's presence and sweet touch in my life. He has a great, big heart of gold and I am blessed to call him my friend.

During my time at Central Michigan University, there were a few others who significantly impacted my journey. Aaric Guerriero first invited me to participate in the coming out panels that ignited my love for sexuality and gender work. Aaric has a personality and witty sense of humor that totally clicked with mine and we became good friends over the years. On more occasions than I can count, we laughed together until we couldn't breathe. His willingness to be open and share his story - and to help others tell their stories - was inspiring to me and helped me to overcome any fear or hesitation I had about coming out to a room full of strangers. Aaric's invitation and encouragement to get involved in the speaker panels was a beacon on my path to eventually delivering my message to the world. I am incredibly grateful for his continued friendship, for his Light in the world, and for the influence he has had on my Journey.

While at CMU, I was fortunate to work in a department where I not only had out colleagues, but where I was supported and encouraged to be involved with the work of the Office of Gay & Lesbian Programs. Laurie Braden became a dear friend and professional mentor who, through her own visibility, provided a space for myself and other colleagues, including graduate students and even undergraduate students to stand in their own authenticity in a professional environment. She has gone on to shine her beautiful Light across her profession as a leader in her national association. I am so grateful to have had the opportunity to work side by side with her and for her courage to live life out loud that ignited my willingness to do the same.

As I share in this book, my time in Athens, Georgia has been probably the most magical time in my life thus far and that had everything to do with the incredible people who were put in my path. I could easily write another book just naming all of them, so I will only mentioned a few by name. Beginning with Dr. Melissa Shivers and the members of her search committee who saw something in me that they recognized was just right for UGA, my experience at Georgia was destined to be charmed. Melissa provided the kind of leadership, supervision, and mentorship that you just don't find every day. Picking up and moving thirteen hours from home to a place where you know no one can absolutely take its toll on a person. Melissa regularly provided a space for me to truly bring my whole self to the conversation and to be vulnerable about the things with which I was struggling and reassured me that everything would be okay. She was a humble leader, who recognized the strength of her team and empowered us to stand confidently in our positions as th resident experts for our areas. I am confident that her leadership style has influenced my own in positive ways.

In the five years that I was at Georgia, I had four different direct supervisors. The day that I learned that Melissa would be leaving us, it was all I could do to get out of the small meeting room without bursting into tears. The only saving grace in that news was that her successor would be Dr. Willie Banks. It was such a mix of emotions having just received the worst news I could imagine, followed up with the best news I could have imagined. By that time, I had developed a strong affinity for Willie. He possesses such a bright and beautiful energy about him and has a way of spreading it everywhere. He made me feel so supported while also fully preparing me for his own eventual departure from UGA. Since then, he has continued his support and encouragement, bringing me to his current institution as a consultant, and being one of the few people to read the entire first draft of this work. He has provided me with words of encouragement and positive self-talk when I couldn't seem to muster it for myself. I love him with all my might and am eternally grateful that our paths crossed when they did.

Another couple that was instrumental to my success in my position at UGA is Dr. Corey Johnson & his husband, Dr. Yancey Gulley. Affectionately referred to as the Gay Mayor and First Lady of Athens, respectively, they immediately opened their home to me when I arrived in Athens. They enthusiastically introduced me to all of the important people in the community, provided me with insight into the history and politics of the city and especially the university. Corey helped me to understand the political power of tenure and Yancey frequently demonstrated the power of a real direct question. Corey and Yancey were well respected leaders in the community and I learned so much from them both in terms of activism and advocacy and their commitment to service to their community. We also became great friends in the process and I cherish all of these things about them.

Most of all, I am honored and eternally grateful for the love and trust that the students who came into the LGBT Resource Center for support placed in me, even when they thought I was just a really nice straight woman. I have such fond memories of so many of them. I had the opportunity to work with such incredible students who were passionate about their community and improving the climate for those who would come after them. Many of them have moved on to become fierce activists and advocates across the country for the LGBTQ+ community at large. I'm so proud to have had the opportunity to love on so many of them and to have witnessed the various circumstances that each of them fought hard to overcome on their journey to being their authentic self.

Soon after I accepted the position at UGA, I received a flood of welcoming emails, the very first of which was from Rev. Renee DuBose who was the pastor at Our Hope

Metropolitan Community Church. I am grateful for Rev. Renee's commitment to the Athens community and that Spirit led her to send me such a prompt and inviting message. I am confident that the timing of the arrival of that email message was Divine and that God worked through her to help, once again, guide me gently on my Journey to exploring my own connection with Spirit. I am also eternally grateful for the congregation at OHMCC who embraced me with love and open arms, and as I share in my story, taught me so much on my Journey.

As a result of connecting with Our Hope MCC so early in my Athens experience, I was also blessed with the opportunity to meet Rev. Dr. Troy Perry, founder of the Metropolitan Community Church denomination, in 2009. He told the story of the founding of the church and I was mesmerized. I was overcome with emotions as I listened intently and realized all that this man had overcome to provide a space for people like me to connect with God. Had it not been for this man being connected directly to Spirit and having the courage to do something even his friends weren't necessarily sure was a good idea, tens of thousands of us around the world would not have a safe place to worship and explore our own connection with Spirit. I am eternally inspired by his dream that he brought to fruition and forever grateful for the priceless gift he has left the world in his church.

While I'm on the topic of high-profile people, I want to

express my gratitude for a few people that don't know me at all. When I was first beginning to explore my sexuality in the mid-1990's and was being met with objection after objection by my family and as a result not feeling generally safe in the world, there were very few people in mainstream media who seemed to be like me. At the time, Ellen DeGeneres, Melissa Etheridge, and k.d. lang were really the only mainstream celebrities who were visible representations of what a lesbian looked like and this has made them influential in my world. As a lover of music, Melissa Etheridge's album, *Yes I Am* was on repeat on my CD player and "Silent Legacy" became my "coming out song." Despite never really watching her show otherwise, I secretly watched the famous episode of Ellen's sitcom in which she came out. I sat in our family's living room, volume turned down as low as I could and still hear it and remote tightly in my hand in case my mom came in the room and I needed to quickly change the channel. These women were trailblazers who have left their mark on the world and on a whole generation of queer people and for that, I am eternally grateful. They were a symbol of validation. What I was, was legitimate. I was not crazy. I was real. I cannot imagine my coming out experience without them. They are some of the very people to whom this book is dedicated.

Sonia Leigh, who is a celebrity in her own right, is another woman who has continuously inspired and motivated me to continue to follow my dreams. I was introduced to

Sonia Leigh and her music during my first year in Athens and was immediately smitten. Her sound resonated with my Spirit and I was taken with her energy that seemed to awaken my inner badass - which I believe we all have. I never missed an opportunity to see her perform live. I became a loyal fan and member of her Facebook fan club, aptly named Fam O'Leigh. At her performances, her endearing Spirit beamed from the stage and filled the room with love for all of the people who had come to support her. I followed her journey on social media and learned more about her story of following her heart and doing what she loved and felt Called to do in the world. While fame and fortune is certainly something just about everyone aspires to, for her it seemed to genuinely be all about the music she was bringing to the world. When I learned that she had left home at the age of 18 with just her guitar and all of her belongings that she could carry with her to pursue her dreams of a music career, I was in awe of her courage and commitment to her passion. Especially when in recent years, that courage and commitment manifested itself in an opportunity to share the stage with one of my heroes - and hers - Melissa Etheridge. Over the last few years, as I have often struggled to find the courage to fervently chase my own dreams, Sonia Leigh has been a living, breathing example of what can happen when we do follow our heart and has been an ongoing source of inspiration on my Journey. Thank you, Sonia, for inspiring me to keep chasing the dream and for blessing the world with kickass music.

Similarly, I want to acknowledge and express my gratitude for all of the lightworkers and healers who continuously shine their Light in the world despite the skepticism that, although seems to be dissipating, is still pervasive. In the same way that my favorite queer icons lent validation to my coming out experience 20 years ago, this community continues to lend validation to my Spiritual coming out experience. The various energy healers and intuitives who have provided insight and healing for me have been placed Divinely in my path and continue to help me grow deeper in my relationship with Spirit. I see you and I appreciate you. Keep shining your Light. The world desperately needs you.

Jennifer Perry, I am convinced that the Universe summoned us to Wyandotte so that I could connect with you and your dream, which has helped me to birth mine. I wholeheartedly believe you are helping lots of others to birth their dreams as well, as you provide a space for people to connect with Source and transform their lives at 359 Degree Yoga. The energy and community of healers you have attracted is healing the world every day. Thank you for answering the Call. Keep taking care of the Universe and the Universe will keep taking care of you.

As I embarked on the writing part of my Journey, Spirit blessed me with a whole other set of angels; people who have specifically helped me along my way with the birthing of this book. Early in the process, I connected with a kindred spirit who was also working on a book of her own. Both members of a self-publishing program, our first assignment was to find an accountability partner. As I scrolled through the spreadsheet of names and descriptions of topics people were writing about, I was cautious about choosing someone who might be a conservative Christian who would not be down with my message. Mikhael Star jumped off the page at me - first, because her last name is Star and I've always loved stars and am pretty sure at some point in my life I wished my first name was Star. But, more importantly, she was open about her life with her wife and family and I thought, "She's my girl!" I sent her a message and the rest, as they say, was history - or as I like to say "herstory."

This led to a two year friendship of weekly calls to check in with each other about the status of our projects. More often than not, it was more of a private mastermind where we provided a space for each other to work through some ideas and thoughts about our books. About six months in, Ethan and I visited Mikhael and her family on our way home from a conference in Vegas. During those few days, Mikhael shared sacred spaces with us in Sedona, AZ. She took us each through a healing medicine wheel ceremony, and I received messages from the Universe that I still remind myself of daily. Perhaps most valuable to my writing journey was a call in which Mikhael gave me feedback based on her first read through of the book. I cried tears of gratitude that day as my

Spirit let me know the feedback she was sharing was spot on. I also found in her, another person with whom I can have in-depth "woo woo" conversations and that makes my heart so happy. I am blessed by her friendship, love, and encouragement.

In the spring of 2017, my friend Nikki Tobias connected me with a book coach, Amy R. Brooks of VoicePenPurpose Publishing, who was looking for writers who were willing to be coached on her podcast. Feeling stalled on the book I had been trying to work on, I agreed to be coached on her show. The conversation was full of energy and provided me with some fresh ideas about how to frame my book. I began following Amy on social media and a few months later, participated in a free online workshop she was offering and that was truly the official start of this wild ride to birthing *Divinely Queer*. I am grateful for the connection that Nikki made for us and will be forever indebted to Amy for her role in helping to finally birth this book. From the continuous challenge and support throughout the year we've spent together to the absolutely magical, once in a lifetime experience of a Costa Rican writing retreat, you have brought me so many blessings and you will forever hold a special place in my heart. Thank you for the amazing work you're doing in the world by loving and supporting women into authorship.

I also want to thank my dear friend Emily Haase for the amazing photo on the cover of the book. We did a shoot about a year ago of photos for my website and never in a million years did I anticipate the cover of my book would come from that shoot. However, I do believe that the Universe conspired with us to get the perfect shot for a beautiful book. Thank you for your creative eye, for your photography skills, and for your generous heart.

To Aunt Sandy and all of my friends who raised their hand several months ago when I asked who would like to be the first to read my book - and then really read it - your contribution to the final version of this book has been more significant than you could ever imagine. Thank you so much for making the time to not only read, but to also offer your feedback. It has made all the difference in the world to the way the story is told and how effective and impactful it will be to readers. I appreciate you all so much and can't wait to send you a signed copy.

Finally, I saved the Best for last. It feels impossible to find the words to effectively express the meditations of my heart when I think about all of the reasons that I am grateful for my husband, Ethan. When you came back into my life in 2011, it was like my whole Universe shifted. Falling in love with you felt akin to the first time I had an orgasm after years of thinking I already had. I realize this is a bit of an odd analogy, but I know you well enough to know you won't mind.

An orgasm is the kind of thing that no one can really, effectively describe to you what it feels like. It's the kind of thing that can only truly be fully understood through experience. When we start having sex, all we have to go on is what it looks like when other people have sex or what other people have told us it feels like. So, in my mind, I was doing the thing and however it felt was how I thought it was supposed to feel because, well, how would I know any different? Until I did. And then it was like, "OH! *That's* what it's supposed to feel like!"

I feel like our relationship felt the same way. For years, I had been in relationship after relationship, convinced on more than one occasion that they were "the one." I had seemingly experienced all the romantic things people talk about when they talk about falling in love. Inevitably, relationship after relationship would end and I'd find myself moving on to the next that was better than the one before and so the new one must be "the one." Then, when I finally decided to stop looking for "the one," you showed up and before I knew it, I had that "OH! *That's* what love is supposed to feel like!" moment.

Suddenly, I understood the desire for people to commit the rest of their lives to each other. For the first time in my life, nothing felt more meaningful and purposeful than the connection I shared with another person. However, this wasn't the typical, dramatic, intoxicating rush of new love that always has a way of bottoming out. We both felt it. We both recognized it. Our Spirits felt simultaneously frenetic and calm. We described it as a "pure, calm, rush." There was no sense of feeling like half of a whole, but rather like each of us were more, together. You helped me look at the future with new eyes, and a renewed belief that I could achieve anything.

Then I moved back to Michigan to start my own business. You were seeing the same bright future and clear vision for my business that we'd dreamt up together, but my vision was suddenly clouded with every color of insecurity, self-doubt, and uncertainty I could create and obsess over. My identity had been so wrapped up in my profession that when I left it, I didn't seem to know who I was anymore.

You would continuously try to lead me out of the clouds with your endless reassurance. You'd paint a vivid picture of the amazing things in our future - in my future - and I would continuously be distracted and consumed by fear. I got so lost along the way, stopping for help from anyone who looked like they knew where I was trying to go, exploring other trails to get to the place I was trying to go, or maybe even other places to go altogether. All the while, you held the vision of where I was going...but you could not do it for me. I imagine it may have felt a little like leading me, blindfolded, through the woods with no tools or resources other than your voice to assure me that our destination still existed, that I was going in the right direction, and to lead me out safely. To make matters worse, plenty of days, I was oblivious to the fact that I was blindfolded. It definitely wasn't what you signed up for and it would have been easy for someone else to have thrown in the towel and left me on my own in the woods. I am eternally grateful that that's not who you are.

For the past five years, not only have you never given up on my ability to get to where we set out to go, but you never even ran ahead of me to try to get us there quicker or wandered down some other trail. You stayed diligently behind me, lovingly supporting me, letting me wander and get to our destination in my own time; allowing me to explore but never letting me get too far off the trail. As exhausted and frustrated as you may have been at times, you stayed the course with me, believing that I would eventually find my way out of the trees and knowing in every cell of your being that when I do, it's going to be magical.

You believed those things not so much because of your faith in me as much as your faith in and connection with Spirit. You have always had an incredibly strong direct connection to Spirit that makes you an incredible human to be around. It is what draws perfect strangers to us everywhere we go. It is what compels those strangers to open up and share their deepest, most vulnerable circumstance and it is why those strangers leave their interactions with us feeling lighter, more peaceful, relieved, and sometimes even healed.

You are a conduit for others to Source energy and whether you are intentionally flowing healing energy to me, to our beautiful fur babies, to co-workers, fellow church members, or perfect strangers, or simply being yourself in the world, you are transforming our world daily with the love you emit for everyone you encounter, every day. It's a constant gift.

I know you have your own beautiful bright vision for the impact that this book will have on the world. I hope with all of my heart that you are right and that it gets into the hands of readers all over the world. I hope that every single one of them find healing and learn to recognize their own Divinity. I also want you to know that you are every bit as responsible for all the good that comes from this dream realized as I am. I may have done the writing, but you have done the heavy lifting by continuing to love, encourage, and support me on an emotional, spiritual, and financial level throughout the process.

I am eternally grateful to you for providing the time, space, and love needed for me to go on this Journey. Know that I would never have done it alone. I would never have left the security of my salaried position to take a leap of faith on my own business. It is because of your love and the space you were willing to hold for me to step into my Calling that this book exists.

ABOUT THE AUTHOR

Formerly the Director of the LGBT Resource Center at The University of Georgia, Jennifer Miracle-Best worked in student affairs for 13 years before leaving academia to pursue her dream of reaching a broader audience with her personal story and her ability to engage people in difficult conversations. Jennifer has been praised for her disarming approach to meeting people where they are and helping them to broaden their perspective through various workshops, trainings, and dialogues.

Having a gift for words from a young age, writing a book is something she always aspired to do, but never dreamed she would ever actually accomplish. However, Jennifer recognized her journey to connecting with Spirit as a result of the very identity that others used to try to separate her from God, as unique. Believing in the power of personal stories, Jennifer knew her story was one that needs to be shared. Her hope is to provide those who have experienced similar spiritual violence with a new understanding of their direct access to the Divine and spiritual healing.

Jennifer finds understanding and inspiration in the works of Neale Donald Walsch, Eckhart Tolle, and Rhonda Byrne. She lives in Michigan with her husband, Ethan, and their four fur babies, Lilly, Kit Ten, Pumpkin, and Reese.

You can learn more about Jennifer and her journey at www.JenniferMiracleBest.com.

Jennifer is available for keynotes, discussion forums, and book talks in person and remotely.

VoicePenPurpose Publishing
supports authors who are ready to use their
Voice, pick up their Pen, and step into their
Purpose to change the world.

For more information about
coaching, ghostwriting, or writing retreats,
contact Amy R Brooks
at Amy@VoicePenPurpose.com.

Made in the USA
Middletown, DE
04 April 2019